Bible Study
for Young Adults

COMMUNITY

Living Faithfully With Others

D0064413

Dave Easterling & Robert Warren

Abingdon Press
Nashville

Community: Living Faithfully With Others

by Dave Easterling & Robert Warren

ISBN 0-687-08307-9

This book is printed on acid-free paper.

Manufactured in the United States of America.

99 00 01 02 03 04 05 06 07 08—10 9 8 7 6 5 4 3 2 1

CONTENTS

MEET THE WRITERS

The publisher acknowledges the contribution of David Easterling and Robert Warren to the development process of *20/30: Bible Study for Young Adults* and to this volume. David Easterling is from Lenoir City, Tennessee. He is the president of CMC (Christian Music Connection) and writes for *LinC*, a weekly Christian education resource for youth. Robert Warren, from Brandenburg, Kentucky, has experience in social work and with Christian youth in various settings. He currently teaches high school drama.

In addition to their work during the development process, David and Robert assisted with the writing of Chapters 1 and 2 of *Community* and suggested ideas for Chapters 3 and 4. Lloyd Chester of Dallas, Texas, also contributed to the early development of the *20/30* series. The work of Diana L. Hynson, Joseph A. Crowe, and Tonya M. Williams made this resource possible.

WELCOME TO 20/30:
BIBLE STUDY FOR YOUNG ADULTS

What makes a Bible study contemporary? Is this resource based on a new translation of the Bible? No. Does it ask you to read the scriptural texts? Yes. Will it give all the answers? No. Will it engage you to find yourself, perhaps for the first time, in a timeless Book of Truth? Yes!

What makes a Bible study contemporary? One answer is, "You do." The *20/30* series is offered for post-modern adults who want to participate in and help structure their own discoveries—in life, in relationships, in faith. In each of the volumes of this series, participants will have the opportunity to use their own experience in life and faith to examine the biblical texts in new ways. You will examine biblical images that shape each person's life, including yours, even if we (or you) are not immediately aware that they do.
ing yours, even if we (or you) are not immediately aware that they do.

Image Is Everything

Images are what shape our decisions. We may think or know certain important data that weigh heavily in a decision. We may value the advice and counsel of others. We may find that the stated or implied wishes of others influence what we do. But in the end, it is often the *image* we hold that makes the decision.

For example, perhaps you were deeply hurt by someone important to you—an employer, a friend, even a pastor. You know in your heart that the institution is not to blame or that friendships are based on more than one event. But the image shaped by the difficult experience is that the job, or the friend, or the church cannot be relied upon. You *know* better, but you just have to make a change anyway. The image was more powerful than the reason.

Images are powerful, and they are familiar. In each of the studies in this series, you will encounter a well-known image that will connect your familiar experiences with some basis in Scripture.

You know how important it is to have a sense of support and roots; to have friends and a life partner. *Community: Living Faithfully With Others* introduces you to Scriptures and life examples that delve into intimacy, work, and family relationships, and more.

You have faith, but may also realize that it can mean many things. It is belief or trust, or waiting or moral behavior, or something else? Or it is all those things? *Faith: Living a Spiritual Life* helps you examine your faith and grow as a Christian.

You know what it's like to make agreements, to establish commitments, to give your word and expect to be trusted. *Covenant: Making Commitments That Count* engages you in study sessions that explain a variety of covenants, what happens when covenants are broken, how to have a faithful covenant to care for others and for the earth, and certainly, what it means to have this sacred covenant with God.

You know what it is like to move to a new place, to have to deal with transitions in school or work or in relationships. You have probably experienced changes in your family as you have grown up and moved out on your own. Some of these moves are gradual, just taken in stride. Others can be painful or abrupt; certainly life-changing. In *Exodus: Leaving Behind, Moving On*, you will appreciate learning how God is in the midst of those movements, no matter how minor or how transformational.

Experience, Faith, Growth, and Action

Each volume in this series will help you probe, on your own terms, how your experience links with your faith and how deepening your faith develops your life experience. If you need a prompt for your reflection, each volume has several pages of real life case studies. As your faith and commitment to Jesus Christ grow, you may be looking for ways to be involved in specific service opportunities. Several are listed on page 80.

We hope this series will help you encounter God through Scripture, reflection, and dialogue with others who desire to grow in faith, and to serve others. One image we hold is that God is in all things. God is certainly with you.

HOW TO USE
THIS RESOURCE

Each session of this resource includes similar components or elements:

- A statement of the issue or question to be explored
- Several "voices" of persons who are currently dealing with that issue
- Exploration of biblical passages relative to the question raised
- "Bible 101" boxes that provide insight about the study of the Bible
- Questions for reflection and discussion
- Suggested individual and group activities designed to bring the session to life
- Optional case studies (found in the back of the book)
- Various service learning activities related to the session (found in back of the book)

Choices, Choices, Choices

Collectively, these components mean one thing: *choice*. You have choices to make concerning how to use each session of this resource. Want just the nitty-gritty Bible reading, reflection, and study for personal or group use? Then focus your attention on just those components during your study time.

Like starting with real-life stories about issues then moving into how the Bible might be relevant? Start with the "voices" and move on from there. Use the "voices" to encourage group members to speak about their own experiences.

Prefer highly charged discussion encounters where many different viewpoints can be heard? Start the session with the biblical passages, followed by the questions and group activities. Be sure to compare the ideas found in the "Bible 101" boxes with your current ideas for more discussion. Want the major challenge of applying biblical principles to a difficult problem? After reading the biblical material, read one of the case studies, using the guidelines provided on page 14 or get involved with one of the service learning components, described on 79.

Great Versatility

This resource has been designed for many different uses. Some persons will use this resource for personal study and reflection. Others will want to explore the work with a small group of friends. And still other folks will see this book as a different type of Sunday school resource.

Spend some time thinking about your own questions, study habits, and learning styles or those of your small group. Then use the guidelines mentioned above to fashion each session into a unique Bible study session to meet those requirements.

Highly Participatory

As you will see, the Scriptures, "voices," commentary, and experience of group members will provide an opportunity for an active, engaging time together. The greatest challenge for a group leader might be "crowd control"—being sure everyone has the chance to put his or her ideas into the mix!

The Scriptures will help you and those who study with you to make connections between real life issues and the Bible. This resource values and encourages personal participation as a means to fully understand and appreciate the intersection of personal belief with God's ongoing work in each and every life.

ON ORGANIZING
A SMALL GROUP

Learning with a small group of persons offers certain advantages over studying by yourself. First, you will hopefully encounter different opinions and ideas, making the experience of Bible study a richer and more challenging event. Second, any leadership responsibilities can be shared among group members. Third, different persons will bring different talents. Some will be deep thinkers while other group members will be creative giants. Some persons will be newcomers to the Bible; their questions and comments will help others clarify their deeply held assumptions.

So how does one go about forming a small group? Follow the steps below and see how easy this task can be.

■ **Read through the resource carefully.** Think about the ideas presented, the questions raised, and the exercises suggested. If the sessions of this work excite you, it will be easier for you to share your enthusiasm to others.

■ **Spend some time thinking about church members, friends, and coworkers who might find the sessions of this resource interesting**. On a sheet of paper, write down two characteristics or talents you see in each person that would make them an attractive Bible study group member. Some talents might include "deep thinker," "creative wizard," or "committed Christian." Remember: the best small group has members who differ in learning styles, talents, ideas, and convictions, but who respect the dignity and integrity of the other members.

■ **Most functional small groups have 7-15 members.** Make a list of potential group members that doubles your target number. For instance, if you would like a small group of seven to ten members, be prepared to invite fourteen to twenty persons.

■ **Once your list of potential candidates is complete, decide on a tentative location and time.** Of course, the details can be negotiated with those persons who accept the invitation, but you need to sound definitive and clear to perspective group members. "We will initially set Wednesday night from 7-9 p.m. at my house for our meeting time" will sound more attractive than "Well, I don't know either when or where we would be meeting, but I hope you will consider joining us."

- **Make initial contact with perspective group members short, sweet, and to the point.** Say something like, "We are putting together a Bible study using a different kind of resource. When would be a good time to show you the resource and talk about the study?" Establishing a special time to make the invitation takes the pressure off the perspective group member to make a quick decision.

- **Show up at the decided time and place.** Talk with each perspective member individually. Bring a copy of the resource with you. Show them what excites you about the study and mention the two unique characteristics or talents you feel they would offer the group. Tell them the initial meeting time and location and how many weeks the small group will meet. Also mention that the need for a new time or location could be discussed during the first group meeting. Ask for a commitment to come to the first session. Thank them for their time.

- **Give a quick phone call or email to thank all persons for their consideration and interest.** Remind persons of the time and location of the first meeting.

- **Be organized.** Use the first group meeting to get acquainted. Briefly describe the seven sessions. Have a book for each group member and discuss sharing responsibilities for leadership.

LEADING AND SHARING LEADERSHIP

So the responsibility to lead the group has fallen on you? Don't sweat it. Follow these simple suggestions and you will razzle and dazzle the group with your expertise.

- **Read the session carefully.** Look up all the Bible passages. Take careful notes about the ideas, statements, questions and activities in the session. Try all the activities.

- **Using 20-25 blank index cards, write one idea, activity, Bible passage, or question from the session on each card** until you either run out of material or cards. Be sure to look at the case studies and service learning options. Number the cards so they will follow the order of the session.

- **Spend a few moments thinking about the members of your group.** How many like to think about ideas, concepts, or problems? How many need to "feel into" an idea by storytelling, worship, prayer, or group activities? Who are the "actors" who prefer a hands-on or participatory approach, such as an art project or simulation, to grasp an idea? Write down the names of all group members and record whether you believe them to be a THINKER, FEELER, or an ACTOR.

- **Place all the index cards in front of you in the order in which they originally appeared in the session.** Looking at that order, ask yourself: 1) Where is the "Head" of the session—the key ideas or concepts? 2) Where is the "Heart" of the session in which persons will have a deep feeling response? 3) Where are the "Feet"—those activities that ask the group to put the ideas and feelings to use? Separate the cards into three stacks: HEAD, HEART, and FEET.

- **Now construct the "body" for your class.** Shift the cards around, using a balance of HEAD, HEART, and FEET cards to determine which activities you will do and in what order. This will be your group's unique lesson plan. Try to choose as many cards as you have group members. Then, match the cards: HEAD and THINKERS; HEART and FEELERS; FEET and ACTORS for each member of the group. Don't forget a card for yourself. For instance, if your group has ten members, you should have about ten cards.

- **Develop the leadership plan.** Invite these group members prior to the session to assist in the leadership. Show them the unique lesson plan you developed. Ask for their assistance in developing and/or leading each segment of the session as well as a cool introduction and a closing ritual or worship experience.

Your lesson plan should start with welcoming the participants. Hopefully everyone will have read the session ahead of time. Then, begin to move through the activity cards in the order of your unique session plan, sharing the leadership as you have agreed.

You may have chosen to have all the HEAD cards together, followed by the HEART cards. This would introduce the session's content, followed by helping group members "feel into" the issue through interactive stories, questions, and exercises with all group members. Feel free to add more storytelling, discussion, prayer, mediation, or worship.

You may next have chosen to use the FEET cards to end the session. Ask the group, "What difference should this session make in our daily lives?" You or the ACTORS should introduce the FEET cards as possible ways to discern a response. Ensuring that group members leave with a few practical suggestions for doing something different during the week is the point of this section of the unique lesson plan.

- **Remember: leading the group does not mean "Do it all yourself."** With a little planning, you can enlist the talents of many group members. By inviting group members to lead parts of the session that feel comfortable for them you will model and encourage shared leadership. Welcome their interests in music, prayer, worship, Bible, and so on, to develop innovative and creative Bible study sessions that can transform lives in the name of Jesus Christ.

CHOOSING TEACHING OPTIONS

This young adult series was designed, written, and produced out of an understanding of the attributes, concerns, joys, and faith issues of young adults. With great care and integrity, this image-based print resource was developed to connect biblical events and relationships with contemporary, real-life situations of young adults. Its pages will promote Christian relationships and community, support new biblical learning, encourage spiritual development, and empower faithful decision-making and action.

This study is well-suited to young adults and may be used confidently and effectively. But with the great diversity within the young adult population, not every line of this study will be written "just for you." To be most relevant, some portions of the study material need to be tailored to fit your particular group. Adjustments for a good fit involve making choices from options offered by the resource. This customizing may be done easily by a designated leader who is familiar with the layout of the resource and the young adults who are using it.

What to Expect

In this study Scripture and real-life images mesh together to provoke a personal response. Young adults will find themselves thinking, feeling, imagining, questioning, making decisions, professing faith, building connections, inviting discipleship, taking action, and making a difference. Scripture is at the core of each session. Scenarios weave in the dimensions of real life. Narrative and text boxes frame plenty of teaching options to offer young adults.

Each session is part of a cohesive volume, but is designed to stand alone. One session is not dependent on knowledge or experience accumulated from other sessions. A group leader can freely choose from the teaching options in an individual session without wondering about how it might affect the other sessions.

A Good Fit

For a better fit, alter the session based on what is known about the young adult participants. Young adults are a diverse constituency with varied experiences, interests, needs, and values. There is really no single defining characteristic that links young adults. Specific information about the age,

13

employment status, household, personal relationships, and lifestyle among participants will equip a leader to make choices that ensure a good fit.

- **Customize.** Read through the session. Notice how scenarios and teaching options move from integrating Scripture and real-life dimensions to inviting a response.

- **Look at the scenario(s).** How real is the presentation of real-life? Say that the main character is a professional, white male, married, in his late twenties and caught in a workplace dilemma that entangles his immediate superior and a subordinate from his division. Perhaps your group members are mostly college students and recent graduates, unmarried, and still on the way to being "settled." There are many differences between the man in the scenario and the group members using this resource.

As a leader, you could choose to eliminate the case study, substitute it with another scenario (there are several more choices on pages 76–79), claim the validity of the dilemma and shift the spotlight from the main character to the subordinate, or modify the description of the main character. Break-Out groups based on age or employment experience might also be used to accommodate the differences and offer a better fit.

- **Look at the teaching options.** How are the activities propelling participants toward a personal response? Perhaps the Scripture study requires more meditative quiet than is possible and a more academic, verbal, or artistic approach would offer a better fit. Maybe more direct decisions or actions would fit better than more passive or logical means. Try to keep a balance, though, that allows participants to "get out of their head" to reflect and also to move toward action.

Conceivably, there could just be too much in any one session. As a leader, you can pick and choose among teaching options, substitute case studies, take two meetings to do one session, and adapt any process to make a better fit. The tailoring process can be evaluated as adjustments are made. Judge the fit every time you meet. Ask questions that gauge relevance and assess how the resource has stretched minds, encouraged discipleship, and changed lives.

USING BREAK-OUT GROUPS

20/30 Break-Out groups are small groups that encourage the personal sharing of lives and the gospel. The name "Break-Out" is a sweeping term that includes a variety of small group settings. A Break-Out group may resemble a Bible study group, an interest group, a sharing group, or other types of Christian fellowship groups.

Break-Out groups offer young adults a chance to belong and personally relate to one another. Members are known, nurtured, and heard by others. Young adults may agree and disagree while maximizing the exchange of ideas, information, or options. They might explore, confront, and resolve personal issues and feelings with empathy and support. Participants can challenge and hold each other accountable to a personalized faith and stretch its links to real-life and service.

Forming Break-Out Groups

The nature of these small Break-Out groups will depend on the context and design of the specific session. On occasion the total group of participants will be divided for a particular activity. Break-Out groups will differ from one session to the next. Variations may involve the size of the group, how group members are divided, or the task of the group. Break-Out groups may also be used to accommodate differences and help tailor the session plan for a better fit. In some sessions, specific group assembly instructions will be provided. For other sessions, decisions regarding the size or division of small groups will be made by the designated leader. Break-Out groups may be in the form of pairs or trios, family-sized groups of 3-6 members, or groups of up to ten members.

They may be arranged simply by grouping persons seated next to each other or in more intentional ways by common interests, characteristics, or life experience. Consider creating Break-Out groups according to age; gender; type of household, living arrangements, or love relationships; vocation, occupation, career, or employment status; common or built-in connections; lifestyle; values or perspective; or personal interests or traits.

Membership

The membership of Break-Out groups will vary from session to session, or even within specific sessions. Young adults need to work at knowing and being known, so that there can be a balance between Break-Out groups that are more similar and those that reflect greater diversity. There may be times when more honest communication, trust, or accountability may be desired and group leaders will need to be free to self-select small group members.

It is important for 20/30 Break-Out groups to practice acceptance and to value the worth of others. The potential for small groups to encourage personal sharing and significant relationships is enhanced when members agree to exercise active listening skills, keep confidences, expect authenticity, foster trust, and develop ways of loving one another. All group members contribute to the development and function of Break-Out groups. Designated leaders especially need to model manners of hospitality and help ensure that each group member is respected.

Invitational Listening

Consider establishing an "invitational listening" routine that validates the perspective and affirms the voice of each group member. After a question or statement is posed, pause and allow time to think—not everyone thinks on their feet or talks out loud to think. Then, initiate conversation by inviting one group member, by name, to talk. This person may either choose to talk or to "pass." Either way, this person is honored and is offered an opportunity to speak and be heard. This person carries on the ritual by inviting another group member, by name, to speak. The process continues until all have been invited, by name, to talk. As each one invites another, the responsibility of acceptance and hospitality in the Break-Out groups is shared among all its members.

Study group members Break-Out to belong, to share the gospel, to care, and to watch over one another in Christian love. "So deeply do we care for you that we are determined to share with you not only the gospel of God but also our own selves, because you have become very dear to us" (1 Thessalonians 2:8).

COMMUNITY:
LIVING FAITHFULLY WITH OTHERS

Community is not a word that you will find in the Bible, but it is at the heart of how Hebrews and Christians understood themselves in relationship to God and to each other. It still is.

Many Communities

We participate in numerous kinds of communities, many of which overlap. We are residents of planet earth: a global community. We have neighbors: a geographic community. We speak a particular language and have our own customs: a cultural community. We work outside or inside the home or go to school: a vocational community. We have family and friends: a personal community. We have certain spiritual beliefs and practices: a religious community.

In this volume, we will examine some of the defining elements of community and how we belong to them. We may also understand that we "do community" differently than our biblical ancestors did. The U.S. culture is very individualistic; we pride ourselves on our independence. Many persons believe that not only are we more or less on our own as citizens, but that our religion is a private, individual matter as well. Community expression is secondary.

The Biblical Community

Our Old Testament forebears would never have understood this: they were a theocracy—a nation truly under God. Our currency may bear witness to the U.S. as a nation under God, but the Hebrews, in spite of their great forgetfulness on this issue, did not really understand themselves as individuals and as a people apart from the kingship or lordship of God. For the Hebrews, God was the ruler, the president, the CEO of all of life. If there was a king, the king was just the spokesman for God's desires.

The Christian community understood itself under the lordship of Jesus Christ, and much of their understanding about this new life in the Christian community had its roots in Hebrew law. When Jesus called believers into a new covenant together, he anticipated that they would live in loving interdependence, like complementary members of the same body.

Who Are We in Community?

In this resource, we will look at several different communities through the lens of our faith to examine who we are and how we participate. Session 1 will help us define community, developing the ideas mentioned above.

Session 2 takes a deeper look into the world of friendship: who are our friends, what does it take to make and be a friend, how to cope when friends disappoint. The famous friendship of Jonathan and David will provide one model of an intimate and faithful friendship.

We don't choose our family the way we select our friends, but they are an important source of community as well. In Session 3, we take a look not just at our family of origin, but consider our family of faith as well.

A significant part of our day is spent in some vocational or educational pursuit. We have colleagues and coworkers, fellow students, employees, and others in the community of work and school. In Session 4 we ask: How do we interact with each other supportively and understand all the complexities of the organizational systems that claim so much of our time? In the midst of work and other life responsibilities, we are also encouraged to find a balance between work and play.

Session 5 approaches the subject of intimacy and our interpersonal relationships. We examine the nature of intimacy, physically and emotionally and celebrate the Bible's appreciation for healthy sexuality.

Not all relationships within our various communities go smoothly, and occasionally breaches occur that need attention and healing. Session 6 looks at what happens and begins to address what to do when things go wrong.

After exploring several aspects of community through the biblical experience and our own experience, Session 7 takes a closer look at how we fit in to the whole scheme of things and how to discern what God's plan is for each of us.

Your Study Group as a Community

It may be that your study group will become a new community for you. Several of the other articles in the front of this volume will give you suggestions on how to make the most of your time together. One important suggestion within these sessions is to close with a circle prayer, which is explained in Session 1. The teaching suggestions throughout the study encourage you to share ideas, opinions, and experiences either in small groups or together. The success of your study depends in part on your collective efforts to engage the study and each other openly, respectfully, and lovingly.

Community: Living Faithfully With Others also assumes that the Bible is deeply relevant to our sense of community—our interactions with family, friends, coworkers, other church members, and even strangers. We encourage you to delve with an expectation of discovery and wonder into what God will say to each of you in your class community and then to carry that message into the reaches of your world.

COMMUNITY: THE STORY OF GOD'S PEOPLE

This session will explore the nature of *community*:
What makes a community?

FIRST THOUGHTS

- A community is simply the place where you live. It can be like your neighborhood or your town or your city.
- A community is the people you feel close to, those you care about the most, like your family and close friends.
- A community is people who believe mostly the same things, think the same way, or live the same way.
- A community is people who have the same interests or the same profession, like the artistic community or the music community.

WHAT MAKES A COMMUNITY?

When a group of individuals share something in common, that makes a community. A community may refer to a group of people who have common rights, privileges, interests, goals, laws, culture, language, politics, or religious beliefs. A community may simply be the people who live on the same land, such as in an apartment building, or in a neighborhood or town. A community

START

Getting Started
Introduce yourselves and tell why you have come to a group studying community. What are your hopes and goals for this time together?

First Thoughts
Which of these four ideas of community do you identify with the most? Explain. Do you totally disagree with any of them? If so, why? Describe your idea of what makes a community.

may be defined by demographics such as age, sex, race, religion, church, or species. Any or all of these shared elements may define a community or may simply be a part of its shared story.

A community can be fairly homogenous, with members who have a great deal in common; or very diverse, with members who are more different than alike.

COMMUNITY IN THE BIBLE

World history is replete with how diverse groups of people have formed themselves around essential religious beliefs in order to survive. Throughout the Bible, we see how community and religion are woven together in the tapestry of the history of God's relationship with the Hebrew people.

- Abraham followed God to a promised land and a new home. Through him we trace the beginnings of a nation, the community of the Hebrews.
- Moses called the Hebrews held as slaves in Egypt to leave that land and to reestablish themselves as a nation. Their exodus became the central saving event for the Hebrew people, their religion, and their culture.
- After centuries of alternating freedom and captivity, Jesus became the fulfillment of the promise for a messiah to Israel and for the whole world. This saving event of God is central in the community of Christians.

The story of the Judeo and Christian communities shares common roots and spans thousands of years. It is one continuous story, and yet much change takes place within it: People come and go; leaders and nations rise and fall; there is turmoil, then peace; there is danger, then cause for new hope.

And yet through it all, there is *God*—not just a minor player, but the dynamic central character of the story; the source of the action, and an integral part of the people's lives.

STARTING OVER AGAIN

Read Genesis 12:1-9.

Sometimes we leave one community to take our place in another, or even to form a new community of our own. This was the case with Abram. The Lord God told Abram (later renamed Abraham), "Go from your country and your kindred and your father's house to the land that I will show you" (12:1). In those days, families were typically large, with many relations living very close together and sharing in an inheritance of property and land, generation after generation. Abram was seventy-five years old; he was well rooted in his community, and his place seemed secure. Yet God called Abram to leave his father's family and his land, travel to a strange new land, and start all over again. If Abram would do this, God promised to bless Abram and to make of him "a great nation." God did not tell Abram exactly how this would be accomplished. God just said, "Go."

And Abram went, taking with him Sarai (who later is called Sarah), his wife; his nephew; his servants; and property. Abram journeyed to Canaan, which was already inhabited by other peoples, and God appeared to Abram again to say, "To your offspring I will give this land" (12:7). From there, Abram continued his journey in stages.

Community in the Bible

Without looking up any Scripture, brainstorm what you remember about Abraham and his family, about Moses and the Exodus, about Jesus' ministry with the disciples, and about Paul's missionary activity. What are your early impressions of how these groups formed community and how God was at work? (You will explore these themes more deeply throughout the session.)

Starting Over Again
Read Genesis 12:1-9.
What happened? What was Abram promised? Using a Bible atlas, trace the journey from Ur (Genesis 11:31) toward the Negeb. How far was it? How long might it take on foot with flocks and children in the group? If you knew it would be such a long journey, do you think you would have uprooted yourself to go? Explain.

Describe a time when you left one community and began or became part of another. Why did you make this change? Did you feel that God called you to do so? What did you take along with you? leave behind? What kind of direction did God provide for you? How are we supposed to respond when God says, "Go"? How *do* we respond?

Closer Look

LOOK CLOSER

Read Genesis 12:5-7. God promised to Abram land that was already inhabited by people of different gods and customs. This proved to be a temptation to Abram's people and played a continuing role in their religious, political, and social conflicts and struggles for centuries to come.

Why would God lead Abram into "occupied" territory rather than some place where there would be no threat of conflict with people of different customs and beliefs? Do you believe God shows favor to one people or one nation over others today? Why or why not?

A COMMUNITY OF RELATIONS

What united these people into a community? First, they were an extended family of Abram's relations and servants. They shared the journey and the hope of God's promise of land, descendants, and blessing. They had a common work of shepherding as nomads. They were guided by a faithful and focused leader and by common customs held in the midst of persons foreign to them. They also shared the human traits of a desire for a home, the privilege to work and provide for a family, a yearning for a spiritual life, and many others. In fact, over time, many of the Hebrews' religious practices were adapted from those of their neighbors with whom they also made friends and alliances (Genesis 21:25-34).

HEAR OUR CRY

Read Exodus 1:8-14; 2:23-25; 3:9-12; 4:27-31.

Abraham's alliances did not all hold together. Abraham's descendants became slaves in Egypt, a territory in which Abram, in his journeying, had found protection and prosperity (Genesis 12:10-16; 13:1-2). Sometimes what pulls a community together is a common burden, the challenges that burden presents, and the people's response to those challenges.

Once again, many generations later, the Hebrews entered Egypt during a famine. Eventually, the Israelites' growth and prosperity came to threaten Egypt. The Egyptian ruler Pharaoh imposed on the Israelites a ruthless and brutal regime of oppression that included forced labor, harsh punishments, and later, murder (Exodus 1:1-22).

Under the weight of their terrible burden, the Israelites cried out for help. God heard their cry and raised up Moses and his brother Aaron to lead the people out of Egypt to their own land, which they had yet to fully receive. After their deliverance from Pharaoh, God provided through Moses laws that would give the people a framework for living—the Ten Commandments (Exodus 20:1-17).

A Community of Relations
What pulled Abram and his travelers together as a community? Which of those elements are common to any community to which you belong?

THE DEVIL YOU KNOW

The trip to the Promised Land was not a smooth one. Numbers 11 picks up the Exodus journey at a place that came to be called Taberah. Once again the cry of the Israelites came to the attention of God, but it was a complaint against God and Moses' leadership. Yearning for the abundant food in Egypt (and forgetting about their enslavement), the people griped that all they had to sustain their strength was that boring manna (Exodus 16). Better that they had remained in Egypt.

Moses was so exasperated that he confronted God: Either help me with these gripers and complainers or kill me quickly (Numbers 11:10-15). God helped, Moses was reassured, and the journey continued.

What made these people a community? A shared burden, certainly, and the all-too human penchant to complain. They shared common laws and boundaries for organizing their society, including worship. They also shared fears: that they would starve or die of thirst, that they would not see the fulfillment of God's promise, that God would not see them through.

SMALL GROUP

Hear Our Cry
Divide the eight Scripture references among different volunteers or teams. Look up the passage, then piece together the situation of the Hebrews. Where do you see the activity of God? Where do you usually turn in times of trouble? Have you bonded with others because of a common burden? What was that situation? How did your community form and function?

SMALL GROUP

The Devil You Know
Have a volunteer read Exodus 16 and report the background information; then read Numbers 11. Choose one person to take the part of Moses, another of God, and the rest of the Hebrews. Act out dramatically or as readers' theater what took place in the wilderness. (You can paraphrase the text first, as well). What pulled the people together into a community?

What were the Hebrews complaining about, and what happened? Think of a time in your own experience when your fears or disappointments were at the root of severe complaining. Did you have company? Have you formed or joined a community, even temporarily, for any of the same reasons as the Hebrews? What happened? How did you feel about it? What place, if any, did God have there?

The Promise Fulfilled

In teams of three, look up **Matthew 5:1-12, Luke 4:14-22, John 15:1-11**. Then together, put in your own words the vision Jesus had for his disciples and for God's community. What made the disciples a community? Of those cohesive elements, which has the greatest appeal to you? the least appeal?

Use the case "Follow Me" on page 75, to explore the formation of a community around a strong and compelling leader, or share the experience of one or two group members who have had a similar experience.

THE PROMISE FULFILLED

God did see the Israelites through. Centuries later, after the ups and downs of captivity by and freedom from neighboring nations, the Hebrew prophets preached that God would bring them a messiah who would usher in a new age of peace and vindication of Israel from their enemies.

We know this messiah as Jesus Christ, who lived in and around Galilee, called his inner circle the twelve apostles, and gathered numerous other disciples. Jesus proclaimed a common vision for life: that those who were denied the benefits of society would be blessed and restored (Matthew 5:1-12; Luke 4:14-22). Jesus drew on his own religious heritage of the Hebrew Scriptures for this vision.

Jesus, with the disciples, lived out this vision by preaching, teaching, healing, and calling forth others to accept that the kingdom of God had come. Its abundance was theirs if only they would see and believe (John 15:1-11).

What made Jesus and his followers a community? A shared vision and shared work to accomplish that vision made their community a reality. The disciples lived with Jesus knowing (if not fully understanding) that he would die for his efforts. Though they faltered, they bore together the death of an intimate friend and carried on this calling. Together they became the first Christians. Like Jesus, many of the disciples were later martyred for their beliefs.

A CHRISTIAN COMMUNITY OF FAITH

Since then, we know that millions of persons have come to see and to believe. But first that early community of faith had to take its beginning steps without Jesus. Led initially by Peter, the first Christians (who saw themselves as Jews who accepted Jesus as the messiah) gathered the believers together around shared goals (spreading the gospel) and shared practices (Acts 2:42). In addition some of them modeled what we could call "Christian communism," that is, they pooled their resources for their mutual benefit (Acts 2:44-47; 4:32-35). As their numbers grew, new leaders emerged.

The apostle Paul carried his gospel message primarily among the Gentile regions of the Greco-Roman world. The Gentiles did not know or understand the radical codes for living that ultimately were based on God's all-embracing love and grace (Matthew 22:34-40).

Paul's evangelistic work was to "preach Christ crucified" and to interpret to new converts the desires of God for a life based on love, which Paul mentioned frequently in his letters. In one sentence, his point was this: "Let the same mind be in you that was in Christ Jesus" (Philippians 2:5). In expanded form, Paul encouraged the new believers to a life of self-giving, generosity, forgiveness, gentleness, truth, and honor (see, for example, Romans 12:9-21, Philippians 4:4-9, and Colossians 3:12-17).

Paul and other early Christians found (as did Moses) that God's way is not always the easy way. For some the Christian life brought with it misunderstanding, resistance, persecution, and even death.

BIBLE

A Christian Community of Faith
In pairs, look at the short references in Acts and one or more of the passages from Paul's letters. What models of community and shared values and behaviors do they reveal? Which touch you the most deeply? Which are the hardest for you to do or need your greatest concentration? What are the benefits to you and to the communities in which you circulate? Why do you participate in a community of faith?

SMALL GROUP

Review the reasons you mentioned for coming together, your goals, and your expectations for this study. Together, write a vision statement for your class, including some of the Christian principles and behaviors that you will work to achieve. Use this as a covenant for your group throughout the study; encourage and listen to one another, discuss issues and feelings honestly and respectfully.

Closing
Throughout the study, consider closing the time together with prayer. A circle prayer gives each person in turn an opportunity to mention an important joy, concern, problem, request for another person or oneself, word of thanks, confession, or word of forgiveness for another. No one is obligated to pray aloud. The group leader might start and finish the prayer or ask for others to assume those roles.

Join now in your circle prayer and include prayers for the welfare of group members and for the covenant you have made.

So why stick with it? What kept these people together as a community? First, they (and we) are a community of faith under the love, wisdom, strength, and guidance of God. We share the conviction that God is the Lord of all that is; that God calls us to be God's people; that through Jesus Christ we participate in a kingdom of abundant life, both here and in the Kingdom to come. We are a people of hope.

A FINAL WORD

One characteristic that brings together the people of faith is prayer. Though our various communities and personal traits may differ, we can be, and are, united by the blessing of a gracious and responsive God. The Hebrews cried for relief in Egypt and complained in the desert. The early Christians devoted themselves to teaching, table fellowship, and prayers, and throughout it all, "great grace was upon them all" (Acts 4:33).

A FRIEND IS A FRIEND

> This session will explore the nature of friendship; what does it mean to have friends and to be a friend?

GETTING STARTED

- A friend is someone who knows everything about you and likes you anyway.
- Friends do what they say they will do.
- Friends like and dislike the same things.
- Friends care as much for my feelings as they do for their own.
- Being a friend means never having to say you're sorry.
- A friend is loyal, no matter what.

EVERYBODY NEEDS A FRIEND

Getting Started

Read the list of statements and decide for yourself which best describe friendship. Explain your answer, and name one friend you have who illustrates the statement you have chosen.

Everybody needs friends; most of us have at least one really good friend. Friendships are as old as history; humans could not have survived alone without a tribe or a clan for support and protection.

We've come some way from the "hunter-gatherer" society, but we still cluster together in some form of community. In a modern culture that seems to prize and thrive on a sense of independence and rugged individuality, why do we open our lives to other people? Why do we look for friends, share our space with colleagues and acquaintances, and search for people with whom we can connect?

Everybody Needs a Friend

Work together to make a list of several qualities you'd expect to find in someone who is a good friend. Then let group members decide how to rank these qualities in order of their importance.

Closer Look

Contrast these two statements:

- Books and friends should be few but good.
- The day is lost if you haven't made a new friend.

Which statement do you agree with more, and why? Locate a Bible with an Apocrypha and look up Sirach 14:6-7. Does this passage seem to support one of these statements more than the other? If so, how?

CAN I BE GOD'S FRIEND?

The Bible clearly records that God has a preferential place for the "little folk"—the poor, the marginal, the alien, the widow—those most vulnerable in their own culture and time. People often talk of God as the Creator, Protector, Lord, and Master—the Almighty. But what about God as our *friend*?

We know that as God's only son, Jesus shared an unparalleled closeness with God and placed a premium on spending time alone with God in prayer (Mark 1:35; Luke 6:12). But throughout history, both remarkable and ordinary people have befriended God and allowed God to befriend them, and some have been quite bold in seeking God's attention and action.

In Genesis, God planned to destroy a city because of its wickedness, and Abraham boldly and successfully bargained with God for a change of heart (Genesis 18).

God spoke to Moses "face to face, as one speaks to a friend" (Exodus 33:11). Recall that when the Hebrews bemoaned their hardships, grumbling against God and against Moses, Moses complained to God on their behalf.

The apostle Paul pleaded with God to remove an unnamed "thorn in the flesh," some ailment or situation that affected him adversely (2 Corinthians 12:1-12).

In the garden of Gethsemane, while contemplating his impending arrest, trial, and crucifixion, Jesus petitioned God to spare him, if at all possible—though at the same time asserting his desire that God's will be done rather than his own (Matthew 26:36-39).

Abraham, Moses, Paul, Jesus—all were leaders in the faith. You'd expect *them* to have a friendship with God—but can *you*? If the life of Jesus Christ and the relationship that Jesus shared with God is our model, then the answer to the question would seem to be—yes!

FRIENDS THROUGH THICK AND THIN

Loyalty and faithfulness are characteristics we prize in friends. The Bible says that "a true friend sticks closer than one's nearest kin" (Proverbs 18:24). One of the most powerful examples of loyal and faithful friendship ever recorded is the story of Jonathan and David.

Jonathan was the son of Saul, the first king of Israel. Saul was a deeply troubled man who had fallen into disfavor with God, and God "was sorry that he had made Saul king over Israel" (1 Samuel 15:35). God asked Samuel to find and anoint another to be king, and God led Samuel to David (1 Samuel 16). Now there were two kings, though Saul didn't know this when David was introduced into his service. This is where David met Jonathan.

First Samuel 18 tells of the beginning of their deep friendship: "[T]he soul of Jonathan was bound to the soul of David, and Jonathan loved him as his own soul" (verse 1). In a symbolic display of devotion and loyalty, Jonathan stripped himself of his robe, armor, sword, bow, and belt and gave them to David. With this act, Jonathan was giving up his own claim to the throne, affirming David as God's chosen king, and placing the lives of himself and his family entirely in David's hands. By freely allying himself both personally and politically with David, Jonathan was also perilously undermining the rule and authority of his father, King Saul.

As David increasingly became the focus of Saul's anger and jealousy, David's and

Can I Be God's Friend?
Form three groups.
Look up **Genesis 18:16-33** (Abraham); **Numbers 11:1-23** (Moses); and **2 Corinthians 12:1-12** (Paul). (If possible, research these passages in a Bible commentary.) For each passage, ask these questions:

■ What is the context?
■ What is the person asking of God?
■ Does this interaction fit with my concept of how people are "allowed" to approach God? How is it different?
■ How did God respond to the person?

Is there anything that we cannot or should not take to God? What, do you think, does it mean for God to have a preferential place for the most vulnerable? Is this the same as having a friendship? Do you think God wants or needs your friendship? Explain.

A Friend Is a Friend

Friends Through Thick and Thin

What are some of the images of friends you see or hear of in popular culture (TV, movies, music, and so forth)? Are those images positive or negative? What do they suggest about the kind of friend you are or want to be?

Describe the friendship of David and Jonathan. Who were the players? What was the context? What took place? Who was in control? What were Jonathan's primary goals in the friendship? What were David's? Which of the two felt the friendship more deeply? Reread 1 Samuel 20:41. Does this change your answer? Why or why not?

How are your friendships similar to or different from the friendship of David and Jonathan? What are your goals in your friendships? In what ways do you make God a part of your friendships?

Read 1 Samuel 18:1-5; 20:12-17, 41-42. What do you think it means that "the soul of Jonathan was bound to the soul of David"? How was God a part of their relationship? Describe your "soul mate," either real or ideal. What is it about this person that you really connect with on a deep, inner level? How is God at work in your relationship?

Jonathan's friendship placed them in ever-greater peril. Jonathan spoke well of David to his father, but the good effects of this did not last. Finally, David, with help from Jonathan, was forced to flee for his life. In a final, heartfelt parting, Jonathan and David wept openly together and recalled the oaths that they had made to each other to be true and loyal friends all their lives and for the survivor to care for the other's family (1 Samuel 20:1-17).

Jonathan and his father, Saul, would lose their lives in battle against their enemies the Philistines. David would go on to publicly gain the kingship of Judah and Israel, forge the greatest religious and political kingdom the world had ever known, and enjoy the glory and honor that otherwise may have belonged to Jonathan. David's true friend, Jonathan, had sacrificed everything he had in order to fulfill God's greater purpose in the rule and glory of David over the Hebrew nation.

A FRIEND-LY CHALLENGE

Proverbs 17:17 says that "a friend loves at all times." This doesn't mean, however, that as friends we agree with, approve of, or even *like* everything our friends do. Being a loving and loyal friend also means confronting and challenging, taking risks for the sake of growth, and being honest.

Proverbs 27:5-6 says, "Better is open rebuke than hidden love. Well meant are the wounds a friend inflicts, but profuse are the kisses of an enemy." This means that though it may be painful at times—for both the speaker and the listener—a real friend speaks the truth in love (as the apostle Paul said in Ephesians 4:15). A person who is *not* your true friend may lack the courage, conviction, or caring to tell you when you are acting wrongly; in fact, he or she may encourage or reinforce your wrongful behavior, or at the least just stand idly by, knowing that you are making a big mistake.

How can you tell who your true friends are? Try asking yourself these questions:

- Who inspires me to be the best person that I can be?
- Who challenges me to grow but doesn't ridicule my failures?
- Who accepts me for who I am but doesn't let me get away with "inappropriate" things?
- Who sees me as more than I see myself?
- Who brings out and participates in my playful, wondrous side?
- Who warns me honestly when I'm about to do something stupid but doesn't walk away after I have done it?
- Who helps me check my attitudes and behaviors to see where I've been and where I'm headed, and what to do if I'm off track?
- Whose advice and counsel do I really trust?

Friends like these can be as close or even closer to us than our family—a sturdy shelter and a treasure.

WHAT A FRIEND WE HAVE IN JESUS

Read John 15:1-17.
We often hear about Jesus' enemies—those who felt threatened by him, those who felt he twisted and violated the law, those who wanted to preserve the status quo. But

Biblical Studies 101: *Hesed*
Hesed is a Hebrew word describing a concept of loyalty that takes into account both *attitude* and *action*. Jonathan talks of loyalty to David, but he also backs it up by making extremely difficult personal and political sacrifices. In what ways is *hesed*—loyalty in both attitude and action—present in your friendships?

CASE STUDY

Use the "Kevin and Stacy" case study on page 76 to explore issues of loyalty in friendship. Or allow group members who wish to volunteer to talk about issues or challenges they have faced in similar circumstances.

SMALL GROUP

A *Friend*-ly Challenge
Form groups of two or three and look at the list of questions to ask yourself. Discuss: Do these questions represent a real inventory of my expectation of a friend and of myself as a friend? What questions would you add? change (how)? eliminate (why)?

Should we expect friends to help us grow emotionally, intellectually, and spiritually? In what ways can this happen?

Turn these questions around and ask them of yourself. (In what ways do I challenge my friends to grow? and so forth.)

What a Friend We Have in Jesus

Read John 15:1-17. Discuss Jesus as the "true vine." How do these statements reveal Jesus' intentions for his friends? How do these images of "vine and branches," "Abide in me as I abide in you," and "lay[ing] down one's life for one's friends" define or identify the bounds of friendship?

Read and compare John 14:15, 21 with John 15:14. What do these verses indicate we must do if we want Jesus for a friend? In what ways has Jesus been—or how would you like Jesus to be—a friend to you in your life?

Jesus brought the early community of believers together in close fellowship; that fellowship later formed the Christian church. What role has the church played in your life—or what role *should* it play—in your friendships and in bringing people together to worship God and to grow in Christ?

Closer Look

Read 1 Corinthians 12. Compare and contrast the apostle Paul's description of the church as one body with many members to Jesus' model of the vine and branches. What are the similarities? the differences? Which of the two do you relate to more? Explain.

Jesus had friends too—good, faithful, loyal friends. Mary, Martha, and Lazarus are mentioned in John 11–12, and we know that several other women participated in Jesus' ministry (Luke 8:1-3).

The disciples—including the twelve apostles—were Jesus' closest friends and followers. As Jesus' faithful servants, the disciples worked side-by-side with him during his three-year ministry of healing, performing miracles, teaching, and preaching the Word of God. The disciples did not always fully understand Jesus' methods or his message, but they were beloved by Jesus just the same and were entrusted with an important place and function in the work of his ministry (Matthew 13:10-17).

In John 15:1-17, Jesus was aware that the time of his earthly ministry was drawing to a close. Surrounded by his circle of disciples in those final hours, Jesus shared one of his strongest and clearest messages about love and friendship. Using a metaphor that the disciples would be able to understand, Jesus described himself as the vine, us—all of humanity—as the branches, and God as the gardener or vinegrower. The meaning of the message was this: *If we stay connected to Jesus, who is from God, then not only will each of us survive, we will all grow and succeed in and through the love of God, each one of us being of benefit to and gaining benefit from the other.* It is because the disciples were finally able to hear, understand, and embrace the full message of God for their lives, Jesus said, that he was able to call them no longer servants, but *friends*.

The remarkable thing is that *we* are disciples too. Jesus' message was not just for the Twelve, but for all believers who follow through the ages: "Love one another as I have loved you" (John 15:12). If we will do this, Jesus tells us, then we will understand the true meaning of friendship.

WHEN FRIENDS LET US DOWN

Read Mark 14:32-42; 66-72.

After the Last Supper with his disciples, Jesus took Peter, James, and John with him to a nearby garden to pray. Knowing that his final hour was near and that he would soon die on the cross, Jesus was deeply troubled. He asked Peter, James, and John to remain awake with him while he prayed. But three times Jesus went a short distance away to pray, and all three times the disciples fell asleep.

Later that night, Jesus was arrested and taken to the home of the high priest for trial. Peter had followed the crowd there and was quietly observing from the courtyard. When Peter was recognized as one of Jesus' friends, he denied even knowing Jesus; Peter did this three times. Remembering that Jesus had warned him earlier that he would deny their friendship (Mark 14:29-30), Peter ran away and cried bitterly, for his heart was broken.

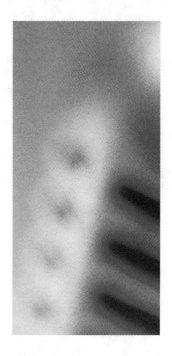

The disciples were Jesus' best friends. They had all vowed to stand by him even if it meant they'd have to die to do so. But in Jesus' time of trial, when he needed his friends the most, they had let him down and left him all alone.

Friends are not perfect. They are human, just like us. They can disappoint us, hurt us, and let us down, and we are capable of doing—and sometimes do—the same things to them.

When this happens, how should we respond? With forgiveness. Jesus reminded the disciples of the important work at hand

DISCUSS

When Friends Let Us Down
Briefly describe a time when a friend disappointed you or let you down. How did you respond to the situation? Now briefly describe a time when you disappointed or hurt a friend. How did your friend respond? Read Matthew 18:21-22. What does this tell us about forgiveness? Which is harder, to forgive or to ask for forgiveness? Explain.

of doing God's will, but he did not blame them for being weak. And after Jesus' death, Peter, James, and John regrouped, renewed their faith, and helped spread the good news of Jesus' resurrection into new life and the kingdom of God throughout the world.

A FINAL WORD

Closing
In your circle prayer, give thanks for friends and friendships. Ask God to be an active part of your friendships and to give you guidance and wisdom in healing broken friendships, strengthening old ones, and starting new ones.

Friends are gifts from God. Friends can be closer than family. Friends are loyal and faithful. Friends are there through thick and thin, and they challenge us when we get out of line. With our friends, we can live, laugh, cry, and love. But like us, our friends falter, they fail, they fall, and they lapse, sometimes hurting us or letting us down in the process.

Yet as Christian believers we have the power and the freedom to forgive, to see the potential of the love of God at work in others, and to reach out to them with the strong and steady hands of Christian love as we build one another up in the body of Jesus Christ.

FAMILY MATTERS

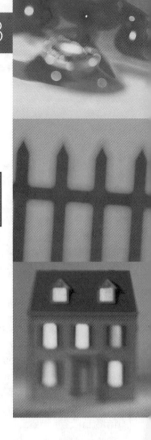

> This session will explore different types of families and what holds them together.

The American family has often been described or portrayed as a mother and father with two or three children, living in a single-family dwelling, and owning a pet. While this model is certainly true for some, it is not the norm. In the U.S. and elsewhere around the world, families may be blended, single-parent, same-sex parents, extended, multigenerational, or multicultural. Also, single persons and their extended circle of close friends can be understood as family.

Regardless of the family configuration, everyone has a role in the family system. Though it is often unconscious, family members will find a way to resist changes in any person's role, because when one person changes, the whole system changes, at least a little bit.

THE FUNCTIONS OF FAMILY

What do we expect from a healthy family? (All families have their idiosyncrasies, so we may have varying ideas of what a "normal" family is, if there is such a thing!) Depending on the family configuration, healthy families

■ model a mature and loving relationship between the partners;

Getting Started
In pairs or trios, take a few minutes each to talk briefly about your own family configuration and what your role(s) seems to be. *It is important for each person to define "family" in his or her own way, not solely in a conventional sense of two parents, siblings, and so on.*

- value the uniqueness of each family member;
- support and love one another through good times and bad;
- teach honest and caring communication skills among family members;
- set and teach reasonable boundaries for behavior;
- teach and model their values;
- challenge one another to grow;
- raise children to be responsible and mature adults;
- interact with other systems in society, such as church, friends, civic groups, and small groups of various kinds;
- contribute to their wider community as good neighbors and citizens.

DOES MY FAMILY DO ALL THAT?

No family is perfect, but healthy families will try to do their best for each family member. One of the joys of the biblical stories about families is that we see them honestly; no glossing over their idiosyncrasies, weaknesses, and failures. More importantly, we see God at work with them, in spite of (or even because of) their frailties. That means there is hope for all of us!

The Interview

Pat has a job interview and has been asked, "What would you like to tell us about yourself?" Pat's family resembles the United Nations: It's blended, multiracial, and multigenerational. Pat has a great relationship with the larger family and celebrates the diversity, but is not sure what this prospective employer will think. If you were

SMALL GROUP

Functions of a Family
In the same small groups, review the traits of a healthy family. Add traits to the list. Then number these traits in their order of importance to you. (Number 1 is most important.) Then, using symbols that you create, rank how well you think your family does. Discuss your numerical ratings, but keep your family assessment private if you wish.

Does My Family Do All That?
Review "The Interview." Put yourself in the place of Pat and decide what you would say (or not) and why. Discuss your opinions and decisions. For a variation of this exercise, consider the question in the context of being at a party where you don't know many people, or at a business lunch with an important client, or at a get-acquainted coffee at your church or civic organization.

Pat, what, if anything, would you say about your family?

FAMILIES STICK TOGETHER

Read the Book of Ruth. In just a few short chapters, we see a whole family drama: a time of hardship, death, uncertainty, fidelity, starting over, educating, planning, honoring, rediscovering love, marriage and children, blessing in the community, and hope for the future.

This is also a multicultural family. Ruth is from Moab; Naomi is from Judah. Moab and Judah were two nations that traditionally had been long-standing enemies. Yet Ruth is immortalized for her love and fidelity toward Naomi and her own native people.

Upon returning to Bethlehem, the two women, who were totally vulnerable without the economic provision and protection of a male head of household, made their way to Boaz, a kinsman of Elimelech. Ruth 2–3 describes how Naomi tutored an obedient Ruth to find favor with Boaz, ultimately leading to their marriage and to the birth of Obed (Ruth 4), who would become the grandfather of David, and thus an ancestor in the lineage of Jesus.

JESUS AND HIS FAMILY

The stories of the infant Jesus and his parents tell us many of the same things about family as Ruth's story, although Jesus' birth was far less ordinary than Obed's.

Read Matthew 1:18-25; 2:13-18; 2:19-23. God intervened for both families in the birth of their sons, though much more intimately with Mary, the mother of the Son of

Families Stick Together
Form four groups. Each group will read a different chapter of Ruth, then quickly pool information to get the whole story. Use a Bible commentary to help understand some of the nuances of the story. What happened? What was the family situation in Moab? in Bethlehem? How would you describe this family system? What are its strengths? weaknesses? How is it like and unlike your own family? Describe briefly an experience of sticking together in your own family.

Closer Look
Ruth 1:1-5 sets up the story in a way that readers unfamiliar with the original language will miss. Look at the definition of each character's name: Elimelech (my God is king); Naomi (my sweetness); Mahlon (listlessness); Chilion (weakness); Orpah (she who turns her back); Ruth (friend). How does the identity of the character shape the story?

Jesus and His Family

Divide the Scriptures among five individuals or small groups. First consider the three brief passages from Matthew. What are the ways in which the angel of God interacts and intervenes on behalf of the Holy Family? What does this tell you about God's family? about God's interest in all families?

Next consider the passages in Luke. What was the place of religious ritual in Jesus' early years (which stayed constant during his life)? What does it mean to you to have an infant (or any and all family members) grounded in your religious rituals?

The Ritual

Consider "The Ritual," which can be a rite of your own choosing. Fill in what details you think are necessary to the case and then discuss how to talk about those important rites within your family. You can act this out as a fishbowl exercise (several people discuss the issue as the family members while the rest of the group observes, then comments) or as a role play in which each person gets an active part.

What purpose does the ritual serve? What does it mean to you to change or adapt your observance versus keeping it unchanged? What other rituals do you observe that help give the family cohesion and meaning? How important is it to you to participate?

God. God intervened many more times to ensure the safety of the infant Jesus. First, an angel declared to Joseph that Mary would have a son. After the birth and the visit by the Magi, an angel warned Joseph to flee with his family to Egypt to protect the baby from King Herod. When Herod died, an angel advised Joseph and his family to return to Nazareth.

Now turn to Luke's reports. Luke 2:21-24 tells of Jesus' first visit to the Temple. The ritual laws of Judaism required the parents to have their sons circumcised as a sign of the covenant God had made with Abraham. A second ritual required that the firstborn male be presented to the Lord and a sacrifice be offered.

Luke then leaps ahead twelve years to report another visit to the Temple (2:41-52) for the festival of the Passover. Hebrew parents had an obligation to teach their sons the law (all education was religious education) and to pass on a trade. Though the circumstances of this story are remarkable, it is not at all unusual that Jesus would pursue his religious education. Under his parents' care and God's guidance, Luke tells us twice that Jesus grew in wisdom and in divine and human favor.

The Ritual

A family of which you are a part is about to celebrate a rite of passage [a baptism, graduation, wedding—you choose]. A few family members want to introduce a couple of new customs to the typical way you observe this rite, and the various generations polarize and square off. The disagreement threatens to seriously dampen the spirit of the event. You're about to enter the fray, but how?

JESUS, THE ADULT CHILD

Jesus grew up, and he had his own notions of family. The Scriptures give us glimpses of Jesus with his natural family and with his disciples, his extended family. When he was about to die, Jesus did what all good Hebrew eldest sons would do: He made provision for his mother. Jesus had brothers; the oldest would have assumed duties as the head of the household. In addition, Jesus attended to the extended family. "The disciple whom he loved," probably John, regarded Mary as his own mother (John 19:25-27).

Jesus had a more expansive concept of family as well. Mark 3:31-35 reports an occasion on which Jesus' natural family members wanted to see him. (There is some ambiguity about why; Mark 3:21 suggests that they feared for him.) Pointing to the crowds whom he was addressing, Jesus announced that his true family were those who do the will of God. This was not a put-down of his own relatives, but an acknowledgement of the more transcendent and broader nature of the family of God.

THE FAMILY OF GOD

The apostle Paul, in his letter to the Ephesians, wrote eloquently about their membership in the family of God (Ephesians 2:11-22). Addressing Gentile Christians unacquainted with the covenants and laws of Abraham and Moses, he assured them, "You are no longer strangers and aliens, but you are citizens with the saints and also members of the household of God, built upon the foundation of the

SMALL GROUP

Jesus, the Adult Child
Do an imagination exercise. Some group members will imagine themselves as Jesus' natural family; others as disciples; others as part of the crowd. As one person reads aloud Mark 2:19b-35, imagine how you would feel about this circumstance and about hearing Jesus say what he did. What does he mean? Do you feel included or excluded by his words? What relationship do you have, expect, or hope for with Jesus? What do these words mean to you now, in your own identity and setting?

BIBLE

The Family of God
Read Ephesians 2:11-22.
Here Paul discusses what it means for this congregation's members to have been outside the Christian family of faith. Not only are they now included, but it means for them a whole new way of life. Use notes from your study Bible or commentary to help understand the passage better. How would you describe the old way and the new way? What is the foundation of this new "household"? "Saints" here refers to living believers, but Paul also includes those who have died in faith. What does it mean to belong to a family with this heritage? As a Christian, you belong to this family. What does that mean to you?

A Radical Family Concept
Read Ephesians 5:21–6:4 against the backdrop of the Greco-Roman family system. How is this teaching radical? What does it mean for household members to treat one another as if all are subjects of Christ? What are the characteristics of such a household? How does this describe your family? your primary love relationship? your relationship with children in your care or of you as an adult child to your parent or parent figure?

apostles and prophets, with Christ Jesus himself as the cornerstone" (2:19-20). Grounding the family unit within the gracious scope of a God of love, Paul went on to expand what for them was a radical family concept.

A RADICAL FAMILY CONCEPT

In the Greco-Roman world, the oldest man of the family had absolute control over his household; his wife, children, and servants all had the same social status—property. A male child never came of age as long as his father was alive. The mother had significant responsibilities in running the household and caring for small children even though she most likely had no formal education. Girls were taught household skills; boys received a more formal education from their fathers, or from tutors or schools if they were available.

All children could be "exposed" at birth, meaning that if their father chose not to acknowledge them, they could be left somewhere for dead. Children who were acknowledged were to be prized, but their father could still exercise strict control over them.

It is in this context that we read Paul's advice in Ephesians 5:21–6:4: "Be subject to one another out of reverence for Christ." Paul then detailed the responsibilities for mutual love and respect for the wife, husband, and children. (He also includes slaves and masters in verses 5-9.)

This passage has been used to support the idea of a wife and child totally submissive to the will of the father (which was essentially the Greco-Roman practice of that day), but this is exactly opposite of what Paul is saying. A man who loves his wife as Christ loved the church is willing to give, even sacrifice, his all for her. A wife who is subject to her husband as she is to the Lord would expect to be treated by her spouse as Jesus Christ would treat her.

Children in the Hebrew and Greco-Roman families were expected to honor their parents. But they were also to be honored, not as objects to be angered, but as children of God. The "discipline and instruction of the Lord" includes those gracious traits Paul had earlier mentioned, for example, in 4:25–5:2: "Be kind to one another, tenderhearted, forgiving one another, as God in Christ has forgiven you." Such radical requirements no doubt gave some of the Ephesian households something new to think about. When Christ is present, life is different!

A CREATED FAMILY

So far, our biblical family models have been mostly of those related to one another. Jesus considered his disciples to be his extended family and friends, but he was not the only one. Paul considered Timothy to be like a son, referring to him as his "beloved child" (2 Timothy 1:2; 2:1). These two had a long history together throughout the missionary journeys in Asia Minor. Paul encouraged Timothy to explore his own gifts and reminded him to claim (and not underestimate) his strengths. Timothy was a teacher and preacher in his own right (1 Timothy 1:3-7) as well as an emissary (1:18-19) conveying Paul's instructions.

Paul used the same familial terms in writing to Philemon about the runaway slave, Onesimus (Philemon 8-16). His practice of mentoring and nurturing was matched as well, for example, by Priscilla

A Created Family
In pairs or threes, spend a few minutes examining these Scripture references for clues to how Paul and the others acted as mentors or extended family members. Then take three or four minutes each to tell a personal story about someone who mentored you. What was the relationship like? What were the benefits to you and to your mentor? Did you ever thank your mentor for the support you received? Do you see mentoring as a way to support those you care about? How do you do that for others in healthy ways?

The New Venture
Read "The New Venture" on page 42 and imagine how you feel about Ronnie's new venture, which so far has not included you in any way. How do you feel about the venture? about Ronnie? about your possibly changing role in Ronnie's life? What would your hopes and expectations be for the dinner conversation?
Then imagine yourself as Ronnie and respond to the questions from that point of view. How might you shape your future together? Have you ever been in a similar situation, from either side? What happened? How did your relationship change? How do you feel about it? What, if anything, would you do differently if you could do it over?

Closing

What have been your own family configurations within your family of origin until now? What gifts, practices, values, behaviors, and assumptions have you learned, held, and practiced yourself? What have you had to unlearn? (Not everything we learn from our family works forever.) Who has been family for you, and how have you established family as an adult? In what ways is your study group "family" to you?

Close with your circle prayer and include prayers for your family.

and Aquila, who took Apollos under their wing (Acts 18:24-26). With their help, Apollos too had his own successful evangelistic ministry (18:27-28).

The New Venture

You have always regarded Ronnie as your "little brother (or sister)" and have been there as a friend and mentor through high school, college, first romance, first job—everything. Ronnie is about to venture out into the world of self-employment in a field you don't know anything about. But Ronnie has been doing "homework," consulting with others in the field, exploring on the Internet, networking with others. Your place has been on the sideline. Finally, Ronnie has time for a breather and this morning invited you for dinner and a long chat.

A FINAL WORD

The family unit is a basic social force in any culture. In the midst of our support for and squabbles with our family members, the family structure seems here to stay. We may define it differently than in the past, but family will always have a future. For Christians, who belong to the household of God, the loving family is forever.

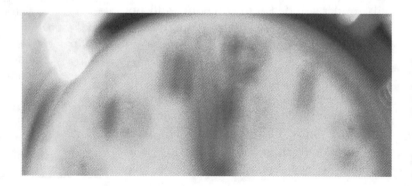

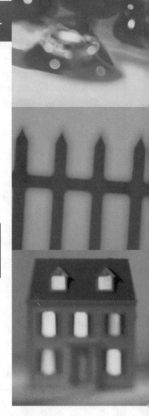

Session 4

WORK, SCHOOL, AND PLAY

> This session will examine the role of education, work, and play in a balanced Christian life.

At least half the day is spent at work or school, or else planning, thinking, and preparing for those times. If you work for pay and attend school too, you commit even more time. Your school and work experience are major parts of your whole community. We work and study with a wide variety of people who have their own concept of justice, fairness, competition, cooperation, motivation, goals, and ethics. Like it or not, they are in your community—and you are in theirs.

THE VALUE OF EDUCATION

The Bible has very clear attitudes about the value of education and about the focus of work. The Book of Proverbs is categorized as Wisdom Literature, which is instructional. It conceives of three types of people: the simple (who have not yet been instructed), the wise (who have heard and who heed instruction), and the foolish (who have heard and rejected sound teaching).

Getting Started
In groups of three or four, describe what are the least and most satisfying parts of your work or school day. Who or what makes time enjoyable? Who or what has a negative influnce on that time?

The Value of Education

Form four groups. Two of them will split the passages from "Proverbs." The other two will look into "Jesus in the Temple" and "Paul and the Early Church." Consider these passages in the context of your daily "work," whether that is employment inside or outside the home, school, parenting, a home-based business, or other endeavor. When small groups have researched their passages, come together to compare your findings.

For **Proverbs,** ask: What are the main points? What are the consequences of failing to take heed of wisdom? What implications are there for one's future? for one's family? How might you put these proverbs in your own words? Are they true for today's culture of work, in its broadest sense? Explain.

For **Jesus**, ask: What do you think is the most significant detail of this story? What does the story tell us about Jesus' priorities and his search for identity? How would you describe the interaction between Jesus and the teachers? Who are, or have been, your best and favorite "teachers" (in school or out)? In what ways is "being about your Father's business" a part of your daily work?

For **Paul,** ask: What is the purpose of work? of teaching or mentoring another person? What are the standards of excellence that you assume in your own work? What sense do you have of how the quality of your work affects others who follow up or have a later part in work that you do? Does a sense of honor or of shame have any bearing on your own standards for work? Explain.

Proverbs

This instruction is intended to teach a young man (in that setting) how to live as an effective, faithful adult who contributes positively to his society. He learns how to be a responsible adult. Consider these Wisdom teachings:

- Value and avail yourself of wisdom (Proverbs 4:13; 6:20-23; 9:9-10).
- Laziness leads to ruin (Proverbs 6:6-11; 10:26; 14:23; 15:19; 18:9; 21:25).
- Rejecting wisdom is foolhardy and leads to shame (Proverbs 10:14, 17, 23; 11:16; 12:1, 8, 15).

Jesus in the Temple

These educational precepts would have been familiar to Joseph as a basis and requirement for instructing his young son, Jesus. But Jesus also took on the responsibility himself. As a twelve-year-old, Jesus remained behind in Jerusalem after a festival in order to converse with the rabbis or teachers (Luke 2:41-52). His parents were frantic when they realized he was not with them on the return home. After three days, they found Jesus in the Temple "sitting among the teachers, listening to them and asking them questions" (2:46). Jesus was an obviously exceptional child, for Luke records that "all who heard him were amazed at his understanding and his answers" (2:47). He explained to his parents that he was about his father's (God's) business. The Scripture adds that he grew in wisdom, in years, and in divine and human favor. Even at this early age, Jesus was shaping his identity and exploring his sense of call through his search for Godly knowledge and his willingness to exchange ideas with and learn from others.

Paul and the Early Church

Other New Testament passages support the belief that one principle goal of adults' work is to advance the faith. This might be done through preaching and teaching; it might also be accomplished by being an honest businessperson. Paul, in Acts 20:29-35, pointed out the importance of his earning his own keep and that worthy work should support the weak. He later counseled Timothy to do his best work, as he had been taught, so that he would never need to be ashamed (2 Timothy 2:1-7, 15). One reason for such care was that Timothy's inherited teaching must be shared with others who would also teach it to still others. What we do in our work affects the quality of those whose work comes after ours.

Clearly the Bible teaches that work has a high purpose and we must prepare for it. In the New Testament, most work is for the sake of the gospel and the kingdom of God, which elevates it from a mere job to a godly call for which commitment and sacrifice are expected. This sense of call is also appropriate, possible, and—from the faith perspective—desirable, for any educational or vocational endeavor you pursue.

CALL AND VOCATION

Call refers to the perception that God or Christ has personally summoned you to repentance and salvation, and in obeying, to work for the good of the Kingdom. Pastors often refer to their decision to enter professional ministry as heeding a call from God. But *call* does not only pertain to clergy. Christians believe that God has endowed all of us with particular gifts and talents and that these capabilities are to be used for the good of the community and, ultimately, for the

Call and Vocation
Turn to "The Malcontent" on page 76 to introduce the subject of call and vocation.

If you choose not to use the case, discuss these questions: How would you define *call* and *vocation*? Do you see your own daily activity as a vocation or something to which you were called? Do you see your daily work as a means to an end, as "doing time," or as somehow separated from your personal relationship to Christ? Explain.

Closer Look
Have you ever felt called by God for a vocation in professional ministry? Have you ever considered how your gifts and skills could be used in a specialized ministry within the church? If so, consult with your pastor for advice on how to explore that call further.

Kingdom. When we do right by our neighbor, we have also done right for the Kingdom.

Vocation is essentially synonymous with *call* but in modern usage connotes "work with a high purpose." If you dig ditches so that they serve their purpose as well as possible and you live to dig the perfect ditch, you have a sense of vocation. If you are a CEO so that you can gain wealth and power by exploiting others, not only is it not a vocation (or work), it's a sin. How you see yourself as a "Christian in the marketplace" not only helps you identify yourself as a Christian, it helps you interpret what it means to merge your personal Christian beliefs and practices with your attitudes, beliefs, and practices in your school or work environment.

God cares how we use our gifts and always calls us to the highest ground. But how do you find the high ground in the competitive, often cutthroat, world of academia and work?

A COMPETITIVE WORLD

We like to think that the "good guy" reaps the recognition and reward of hard and honest work; but we work and attend classes with cheats as well as with persons of great integrity. In fact, these institutions probably give us the most rigorous forum in which to exercise our personal values and beliefs.

The arenas of higher education and work push us to face

- establishing appropriate boundaries for ourselves and others;
- dealing with authority—our own and others';
- accepting responsibilities and keeping commitments;
- competing fairly in a sometimes unfair environment;

- coping with inequity in pay, respect, and personal treatment;
- working with teams in which some seem not to "pull their full weight";
- deciding how much personal time, if any, will be given to work over the required work hours and how to balance life, work, family, church, and other priorities;
- facing an environment in which rapid change seems inevitable;
- working for employers whose priorities and values may be quite different from our own.

How we address these issues depends in large part on our perspective. What is your perspective about school or work? Why are you going to school, looking for employment, or working? How would you address all the issues just listed? Few persons have the luxury of not having to work for a living, and many are unhappy or dissatisfied in the work they have. Your attitude can range from "I want to save the planet" to "I hate what I'm doing, but I can't afford to quit."

Once you assess your own perspective, it is helpful then to work to understand the nature of the organization that occupies much of your daily efforts.

UNDERSTANDING THE ORGANIZATION

Understanding the company or school as an entity helps us figure out how to fit in with integrity and how to work successfully and responsibly.

- Does the company or school perceive of itself as a community? What kind of person-oriented environment does the institution strive for, if any?

Understanding the Organization
Form small groups so that, if possible, there is a mix of persons who are employed in the workplace, at home, at school as students, in administration and in non-management. Consider the questions in the text. What insight do you gain from the different positions your group occupies in the organization?

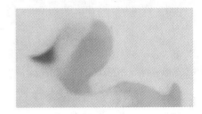

What insight and experience do longer-term workers have for newcomers to the workplace? What insights do new workers bring to longer-term workers? How much accommodating do you have to do for the organization to achieve its goals? What impact does your theological stance about work have on how you spend your typical day? How does your work affect others? What personal or work habits might need to change?

Putting It Together

Do a fish bowl exercise. A volunteer who agrees to examine his or her work situation will be interviewed by a second volunteer. Others observe silently, then offer feedback from the interview.

Interview questions: How would you rate your work satisfaction? What is your understanding of the work culture and how you fit in it? What gifts do you have for your work? What are your weaknesses? Do you have a sense of vocation about why you do what you do? Why or why not? If all barriers were removed, what would be your ideal work?

- How are people treated? What does that say about the persons in authority? about the others?
- Who's in charge? Who has the power "on paper" and who has it in practice? Who makes the decisions? What input do you have?
- How flexible are the power people? How open are they to new ideas, new people, new ways of doing things? If you are in a power position, how open are you?
- What spoken and unspoken rules are there about how to do business and how to treat others? How are they enforced?
- What are the organization's goals, and how respectful are you of them? How comfortable are you in supporting those goals? What influence do you have on those goals?
- What personal or work habits seem incompatible or unhelpful in that environment? What would it mean to you to change?
- What theological and ethical precepts form the basis of your identity? How well do they fit the corporate or school mold?

PUTTING IT TOGETHER

After assessing some of the biblical teaching about the value of education and work for the community and the community of God, your own perspectives about work or school and why you invest your time there, your sense of call and vocation, and the identity of the organization, you should be well on your way to figuring out the world of work and your place in it. Then comes the opportunity to discern if you're in the right place, at least for now. Is school or work satisfying and meeting your vocational goals and needs? If things feel out of kilter, it doesn't necessarily mean that you're in the wrong place. It could be that you just don't have enough time for play.

THE IMPORTANCE OF PLAY

How do you relax? *Do* you relax? Do you play at work; that is, provide yourself with some moments of lightheartedness and enjoyment with your coworkers? Can you laugh at yourself and enjoy a good-natured joke on yourself? Do you take a regular day off, a day for sabbath and for rest? Do you have hobbies or a variety of pleasant interests? Do you play too much by spending long hours in front of the computer or television?

Jesus knew the importance of joy and recreation. In fact, he was criticized (inappropriately) for it. The Pharisees called him a "glutton and a drunkard" because he came "eating and drinking" (Luke 7:33-35). We know that Jesus enjoyed dinner conversation with many people and took time to attend a wedding (John 2:1-11). Jesus' Scriptures pointed out that "a cheerful heart is a good

The Importance of Play BIBLE
Look up the five short Bible passages. What portrait do they give you of the place of play and sabbath in their own setting? Is this picture relevant today? Explain. How well do you observe a time of sabbath for rest and worship?

SMALL GROUP
Choose a type of play that most of you enjoy, or form small groups for specific interests, such as sports, games, the arts, and so on. What is it about this type of play that engages you? refreshes you? How often do you get to participate? What priority is play or rest in your life? How does it balance with your work life?

A Final Word
What sense do you have that your play is biblically mandated? What might you need to do to have the proper balance between work and play?

medicine, / but a downcast spirit dries up the bones" (Proverbs 17:22).

Sabbath, as it is observed in the Scriptures, is the model for regular rest. Its purpose is two-fold. One is to celebrate God's work of Creation and to rest from one's completed labor as God had done (Genesis 2:1-3). The second is the practical necessity of giving children, servants, even

animals a day of rest, which also served as a memorial of God's release of Israel from slavery in Egypt (Deuteronomy 5:14-15). By phrasing the mandate to cover children, slaves, and animals, that meant *everyone* and *everything* deserved a break from their work—not just God, but all of creation, including you.

A FINAL WORD

Work and school make up a major part of the larger community in which we live and a major part of how we spend our time. It's important to balance in time for sabbath (and worship) and for play. After all, we don't want our "bones to dry up."

Closing
Close with your circle prayer. Include in this time prayers for worthy work, for your coworkers and classmates, and for a deep sense of calling and vocation. If anyone has expressed an interest in a professional ministry, support that calling with prayer as well.

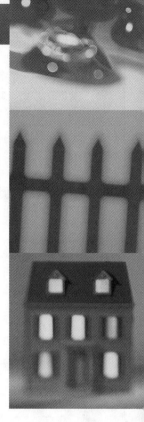

Session 5

INTIMACY

This session will explore the nature of intimacy within the Chrisitan faith.

WHAT IS INTIMACY?

Just what is intimacy? How would you define intimacy? How do you show intimacy? In this session we will explore issues of intimacy among close friends and between couples.

Intimacy involves a whole host of dynamics: honesty, trust, fear and risk, self-revelation, and devotion, for example. We find and establish intimacy on several levels: the physical, intellectual, and spiritual, to name three. It is possible to have an intimate relationship that is not physical in any way, but that joins in a powerful way an appreciation, even passion, of another's soul.

Loving sexual intimacy unites two people who demonstrate not only a healthy sense of their own self-identity, but a physical unity and communion with each other. For some persons, "being intimate" is much more of a physical than an emotional bond; sometimes emotional intimacy is not a part of sexual or other physical intimacy at all. As a broad generalization, men may experience intimacy first physically, while women attach themselves emotionally first. In any case, men and women frequently view intimacy in different ways, and misunderstandings or differing attitudes, desires, needs, and practices can be a point of conflict.

Getting Started
Please Note:
Conversation about intimacy is sometimes problematic in a public forum such as a study class. This session will suggest topics and questions of a personal nature that you can explore during the session, but may want to deal with in a protected setting with others of your choosing.

In pairs, describe in just one or two sentences how you define intimacy.

What Is Intimacy?
Look at some of the dynamics of intimacy; what others can you add? Is intimacy, for you, more physical, emotional, or spiritual? If one aspect seems more important to you, what, do you think, is an appropriate balance of the three? What experience do you have with an intimate, but nonphysical, relationship?

In the Bible, the first man and woman, created by God in God's image, are described as being of the same flesh: "Therefore a man leaves his father and mother and clings to his wife, and they become one flesh" (Genesis 2:23-24).

Closer Look
In a protected setting, discuss: How would you define physical intimacy? sexual intimacy? Do you think there is a difference? If so, what is it? Have you and your partner argued about or misunderstood the other's concept of intimacy? What did you do to try to understand each other better? What do you do now if you disagree or have conflicting desires?

"BECOMING ONE FLESH"

"Becoming One Flesh"
Read Genesis 1–2, paying particular attention to the creation of the man and the woman. Note that the creation process differs in the two Creation stories. What was the relationship between the man and the woman according to God's plan in Creation? What does "the two became one flesh" mean to you?

First, note that the one flesh Adam and Eve become is not just his or only hers, as if one has subsumed the other. "One flesh" means being one in mutual loyalty, in mutual affection and sexual expression, and in producing and caring for children.

In healthy relationships, each individual is respected, loved, and treasured for the uniqueness that he or she brings to the relationship. But the two together have an identity as a couple that they don't and can't have as two single people. Each understands and adapts to mutually accepted roles. One's life is intimately intertwined in the life of the other through the sharing of mutual dreams, goals, hopes, successes and tragedies, foibles, illnesses, conflicts, triumphs, and the dailiness of life.

What makes for such mutuality? Must each person in an intimate relationship agree with the other, never squabble, hold identical views and values, unquestioningly accept the other's behavior and attitudes? No; mutuality is not the same as conformity. Mature mutuality is dependent, in part, on the healthy self-worth of each partner, who then can affirm the identity and roles of the other without losing his or her own valid sense of self.

HEALTHY DESIRE

The Bible is very clear in its affirmation of physical intimacy as a natural and normal part of life. Song of Solomon, also known as Song of Songs, is a series of love poems between a man and a woman who describe each other as "my beloved." Each one extols the beauty of the other (Song of Solomon 5:9-16; 6:4-10, for example) and expresses great eagerness to be together (3:1-5).

The poem is very sensuous and uses numerous metaphors for sexual activity and desire, such as the woman's invitation: "Let my beloved come to his garden / and eat its choicest fruits" (4:16c) and the man's response: "You are stately as a palm tree, and your breasts are like its clusters / I say I will climb the palm tree and lay hold of its branches" (7:8a). Sensuality, sexuality, and sex are good, the Bible affirms, when all are mutual and loving.

RISK

That's the risk we take when we open ourselves to someone else: Will I be treated respectfully and lovingly? Intimacy does not exist without risk; risk without hope or expectation of honesty and trust is often avoided. Intimacy is threatening to someone who has not established the ability to trust

DISCUSS Do you know of relationships in which the "one flesh" is principally one person's? What is the effect of that kind of unity? How do you understand healthy mutuality? What does it mean to have an identity as a couple? What, in your experience, is the importance of uniformity of values, views, and so on in an intimate relationship? of unity? of harmony?

BIBLE

Healthy Desire
Read the selected passages in Song of Solomon. Among several theories, some commentators regard this as an allegory of God's love for Israel, others see it as a wedding song, and still others interpret it in different ways. What do you think about having this sensuous writing in the Scriptures? What does it say to you about the faith community's regard for sensuality, sexuality, and sexual activity?

SMALL GROUP In pairs or threes, discuss these ideas. Our society often gives mixed messages about physical intimacy, ranging from some variation of "Sex is dirty; save it for the one you love" to "If it feels good, do it." What image do you hold? What idea do you want your intimate partner to have? What message do you think is appropriate to teach your child, when the time comes?

Risk

What, do you think, is the relationship between risk and trust? What other destabilizing factors can you identify?

Closer Look

In a protected setting, describe briefly the intimate relationship in which you felt the greatest degree of trust and the least. Identify the factors that affected your comfort level.

Read the case about Terry and Leslie. What are the issues of risk here? Do you identify more with one character or the other? Explain. Is there any right or wrong in Terry's discussing the relationship with others or with Leslie's keeping everything completely private? Would your answer change depending on the issue they were dealing with? Why or why not? How can Terry and Leslie seek help in ways that are comfortable and appropriate without increasing the anxiety or sense of risk in the relationship for the other?

because intimacy requires vulnerability and self-revelation.

We shy away from risk when our own history in relationships or in our family is one of disappointment. Mom and Dad divorced; so did some of your aunts and uncles. The noncustodial parent made promises that he or she didn't keep. One parent or the other had an addiction to work or to alcohol or to something that impaired the quality of life at home. Friends thought to be sincere turned away or betrayed you.

The list of destabilizing influences a family and its members can face is endless in our frenetic and highly mobile society, and those influences work against the establishment of intimacy. But that hardly means that intimacy is out of reach.

Terry and Leslie

Terry and Leslie are in a solid, committed relationship. Things "work," though the two are very different. Terry is very outgoing and has several close friendships, while Leslie is a more reserved, private person.

Leslie feels that disagreements or misunderstandings in the relationship should be worked out privately between the two of them. Terry needs to turn to various trusted family members or close friends for advice and counsel.

Leslie feels uncomfortable with the idea of other people learning "intimate" details of their relationship. For Terry, this network of support is vital and provides the right kind of encouragement to keep the relationship with Leslie "on track."

HONESTY AND TRUST

Learning to trust is a basic achievement that is essentially established (or not) by about age two. When children do not learn trust, their intimate relationships throughout life are often unsatisfying or unhealthy. When they do, intimacy is not only possible, it can attain tremendous depth.

Some trust busters:

- Constant disappointment
- Broken promises and abandonment
- Abusive treatment, physically, emotionally, mentally, or spiritually
- Feeling "different"; not fitting in
- Withholding love

Some trust builders:

- Constancy; keeping promises
- Freedom to make mistakes without inappropriate consequences
- Sincere compliments; affirmation
- Support through tough moments
- Unconditional love

Ben and Eileen

Ben and Eileen are colleagues and very good friends. Both are married, and the two couples socialize from time to time. Ben and Eileen are very professional at work, but when Eileen was commended for outstanding work by the boss at a recent staff meeting, Ben gave her a kiss on the cheek and a big hug. Eileen always gets her work done well and on time, but she's in Ben's office frequently. Sometimes she makes up a reason to go. Everyone knows they are great friends, and they talk over everything together. So far, no one has said anything about it—out loud.

SMALL GROUP

Honesty and Trust
Review the "trust busters" and add new ones to the list. Then do a ranking exercise. Mark a place in the room as 1 (major issue) and a place opposite as 10 (no big deal). Then stand at the place between the markers that indicates your opinion about how big a problem each of the "trust busters" is.

Then do the same thing for the "trust builders," adding to the list, then standing between marker 1 (most important) to 10 (least important).

Discuss your agreements and disagreements on your rankings. What place does one's faith have in the establishment of trust and honesty?

CASE STUDY

Read about Ben and Eileen. Imagine yourself as the spouse of one of them. If you are secure in your relationship, how might you interpret their actions and react to their friendship? If you are not secure? What issues of trust do you see here? How does little "stuff" become big stuff? What positive factors form the "bedrock" of your own mature mutuality and intimacy?

**When Love
Goes Wrong
Read John 7:53–8:11.**
Note that the main point of this passage is that it is a legal trap for Jesus concerning the application of the law. Use a commentary for better understanding of the legal issue about witnesses, then examine Jesus' behavior toward the woman. What are the boundaries here?

DISCUSS

Boundaries
What are the important boundaries in your own intimate relationships? What boundaries can never be crossed without permanently damaging your relationship? To what extent will you try to forgive unacceptable behaviors and attitudes? What are the measures for how bad it can get before it becomes fatal to your relationship? In your most intimate relationship, what signals or practices are in place that help you keep from getting into crisis?

DISCUSS

Forgiveness
Who should initiate forgiveness, the maligned party or the one who caused the hurt? How do we understand accountability for hurting each other, and what does forgiveness imply regarding change? What are the consequences of failing to give or to receive forgiveness?

WHEN LOVE GOES WRONG

Our relationships may veer "off track" or falter seriously, and one major source of trouble is unfaithfulness. Infidelity can be physical or emotional. If "Ben and Eileen" become so close that their primary allegiance and emotional attachment is to each other rather than to their spouses, they run a grave risk of unfaithfulness, even if they never touch each other. Of course, if they do touch each other intimately, another obvious boundary is violated. A serious breach can, and eventually will, open between the marriage partners, even if Ben and Eileen try to keep their secret.

When (and what) is it appropriate to forgive? Jesus told his disciples to forgive seventy-seven times (Matthew 18:21-22). In this case, seven was seen as a perfect number, suggesting completeness. Jesus' response was not numerical, but superlative—forgive perfectly and completely.

Does this mean that anything and everything should be forgiven? Jesus was also clear about boundaries. A woman caught in adultery was brought before him for condemnation (John 7:53–8:11). Jesus did not condemn her, in part because the Jewish law did not permit it without a sufficient number of witnesses. Jesus' response was gracious, but in saying, "Go your way, and from now on do not sin again," he also acknowledged that not all behavior is acceptable.

TRUE LOVE

Grace is an important ingredient in establishing and maintaining an intimate relationship. Grace is the foundation of true

love—not the fairy-tale kind, but mature, deep love. The Bible helps us see what true love is because it describes the results that will be experienced in the community, not just in the relationship or the household. One's own Christian character sets the stage for what will happen in all relationships.

The Creation stories in Genesis picture the ideal relationship (Genesis 1–3). Men and women were created to be perfect and equal partners to each other and to live in perfect harmony with God. Then came temptation and the Fall. The relationship continued, but with inequality, pain, and disharmony.

First Corinthians 13, for example, sets out standards for the Christian community. If Christ truly is at the center of a person's life, he or she will be patient and kind, not envious, boastful, arrogant, or rude (1 Corinthians 13:4-7). While these beautiful words on love were written to describe a spiritual gift, not to define the nature of romantic relationships, the advice is nonetheless on target. Those standards create a measure for commitment, a gauge of character, and a context in which love and intimacy flourish.

SMALL GROUP

True Love
Just for fun, make up a fairy tale about true love. In groups of four or five, one person will start the story, take it to a transition point, and then the next person will take up the story, and so on, until everyone adds something to it. (It doesn't have to have an ending.)

Discuss the elements that went into the story, and identify how many of them pop up in some fashion in your own intimate relationships. For example, who is the Prince (or Princess) Charming figure? Who or what are the villains? What are your obstacles to "true love," and how do you overcome them?

BIBLE

Read 1 Corinthians 13. This passage is about the greatest of all spiritual gifts: mature, deep love. What are the characteristics of love? Do you think you can attain all of them? Explain. What would your intimate relationship be like if you consistently exhibited the opposite of just three or four of those characteristics? Which, for you, is the most important? the most natural and easy? the most difficult? What can you do to work on the difficult ones?

SMALL GROUP

Sticking With It
Form three groups to consider the models of perseverance we see in various media. One group will consider movies, another books, another popular music. Each group should consider these questions. What are the most prevalent images and messages about:

■ intimacy?
■ when and why to stick together? when and why to give up?
■ the cost of quitting? the benefits of staying together?

When small groups have spent several minutes considering questions, come together to compare your insights.

STICKING WITH IT

Even the most loving and patient people may founder in the rough waves of a relationship. We are inundated with social models of quitting. Couples break up and divorce. Workers change jobs rather than work with a difficult boss. Students take an incomplete. We litigate rather than negotiate. All these options tell us that we don't have to work through trouble; we just work our way around it. But at what price?

■ Failing to face a problem robs us of the experience of searching for and implementing healthy solutions.
■ Moving from situation to situation may prevent us from analyzing why problems or crises arose in the first place.
■ Striking out against another cloaks us from recognizing our own weaknesses and needs to change, take responsibility, and mature.
■ Manipulating or dealing in other "trust busters" undermines intimacy and jeopardizes the ability to recover.

Sticking with it may involve a great leap of faith and a high level of risk, but the rewards can be a sense of completeness and joy beyond description.

A FINAL WORD

Intimacy is scary; intimacy is profoundly good and life-enriching. Intimacy is not dependent on marriage but on relationship. God created us for healthy intimacy with spouses, friends, and God, and God shows us the way.

CLOSE

Closing
Join together in your circle prayer. Include prayers for strength and wisdom for those in secure intimate relationships and for healing and insight for those in troubled or unsatisfying relationships.

WHEN THINGS GO BAD

This session explores what happens when breaches occur in our various communities and some first steps toward healing.

Life is good. Bad things happen. Nothing stays the same. If life is worth living, it moves, grows, changes, endures hurts and setbacks, lurches ahead, offers countless disappointments and innumerable joys. And since we don't usually live in isolation or seclusion, all of these events and feelings occur in our various communities.

How do we deal with the distortions, disappointments, disillusionments, and disasters that threaten to rip us apart and our communities with us? How do we recover and heal? What resources does the community of faith offer to us to make our way through difficulties? Take a look at The Fall.

FALLING HARD

Consider Eden. In Genesis 1–2, God has created all the earth, including the man and woman, whom God has placed in the paradise of Eden to work, live, care for creation, and enjoy the relationship with each other and with God. They were created to do this. It was their "job," and what an enviable job it was.

Then, the serpent entered the picture. Read Genesis 3:1-19. "Now the serpent was more crafty than any other wild animal that the Lord God had made" (3:1). What hap-

Getting Started
Without discussing any of the issues (that will come later), brainstorm and list (1) things that are good about life, and (2) events or circumstances that distort or hurt those good things.

59

pened next was the beginning of an event that would forever change everything God had made. In church lingo, we call this "The Fall."

The serpent, representing temptation, introduced to the man and woman the idea (which was exceedingly appealing) that they could be more than they were; in fact, they could be like God. All they had to do was to disobey God's mandate against eating from the tree of the knowledge of good and evil (see 2:16-17). The woman ate and gave it to her husband. He had a bite too.

After eating the "forbidden fruit," things happened just as the serpent had said. They were aware of good and evil, but the consequence was far from what they evidently expected. They experienced guilt and fear—the first breach of the community that God had created to be very good. Not only that, but God pronounced a curse on the serpent, on the woman (through increased difficulty in childbirth and by submission to her husband), and on the ground (so that the man would have to toil and strain to farm and tend it).

"UN-EATING THE APPLE"

In their ideal world, Eden, childbearing would have been less painful (or painless); the woman and man were equal partners, and the produce of all the earth (except from those two extraordinary trees) was theirs for the taking. Now they were expelled.

None of us can "un-eat the apple," but did that mean that the brokenness the man and woman introduced to the community could never be undone? No, it didn't.

Even in the midst of the curse, there was promise. The relationship between the man and woman would continue and would be based in part on desire. They could expect to have the blessing of children, even though the birth process would be difficult. They were promised food, although farming would not be easy. And then God, who had said they would die for their sin, gave them clothes, a sign of protection and care (3:20). This couple had betrayed and disappointed God, and God held them accountable. But God also loved and provided for them.

THINGS HAVEN'T CHANGED MUCH

Jesus also loved those who betrayed, violated, and hurt others. From Adam and Eve, through all the centuries of human existence, to today and beyond, human beings have and will continue to hurt one another. Things haven't changed much.

Judas, one of the inner circle, betrayed Jesus. Judas was the group treasurer, a position of trust, although John evidently thought him unworthy of it (John 13:29; 12:6). What were the consequences of Judas's actions? Jesus was delivered to death (John 18–19), the Twelve were plunged into chaos and fear (John 18:1-11; 20:19), and Judas's life ended in misery (Matthew 27:3-5; Acts 1:16-20). The disciples would never be the same again. But in some ways, they were better.

Peter, who had also betrayed Jesus (John 18:15-18, 25-27), became a strong and brave spokesman for the group (see Acts 1–2, for example). The other eleven took up the mantle as well and with the power of the Holy Spirit and Jesus' command, were sent to be his "witnesses in Jerusalem, in all Judea, and Samaria, and to the ends of the earth" (Acts 1:8). This "itinerary" covered their religious capitol (Jerusalem), their homeland (Judea), the capitol of their near-

Closer Look
After the story of Eden, we have several other stories that repeat this cycle of brokenness and restoration, with Noah through the Tower of Babel.

Read Genesis 4:1–12:4 and look at a Bible commentary for more detailed information about these events. How did humankind continue to breach and bend their relationships with one another and with God? What did God do? What are God's apparent reasons? What does this tell you about brokenness and restoration?

Things Haven't Changed Much
Imagine that the group is an arbitration panel. Using the Bible references in the text, some will look into Judas's actions and motivations. Others will do the same for Peter. Others will arbitrate the effects of each one's betrayal. Include in the discussion how the faith community worked at healing the damage caused by these betrayals.

Then, citing one of the personal experiences mentioned early in the session (or any other example), discuss how Jesus' or the early church's response to those community breaches serves as a model (or not) for how to cope with contemporary distortions or disasters in our various communities.

Closing In, Shutting Out

Form four groups and divide **James 2–5** among them. Chapter by chapter, review James's charges against the faith community. Based on his charges, brainstorm your own specific list of "small sins" that are similar. If you are willing to confess, mention which of those small sins are personal favorites or those with which you struggle. How do these sins hurt others individually? What is the effect on the community?

When Hurt Hits Home

Form three groups. Each one will consider one of the cases and respond to these questions:

- What are the issues?
- What seems to have happened and how do you know?
- What are the dangers to the community (workplace, family, interpersonal relationship, and so on)?
- What personal responsibility needs to be accounted for? What corporate responsibility, if any?
- What might have been done to avoid the problem?
- What courses of action might be taken in this circumstance?
- What potential promise do you see in the situation?

After each group discusses its case, come together to compare notes. What new insights have you gained into how the community can be wounded and what hope there is for restoration?

est enemy (Samaria), and everywhere else. There was no place beyond the requested reach of the disciples. Theirs was an expansive and successful ministry. Jesus' death did not shut it down; his death and resurrection empowered it.

CLOSING IN, SHUTTING OUT

Sometimes, though, we want to preserve our community—no changes, no strangers, no one not "like me." We actually hurt or distort the community by wanting to keep it just as it is.

Or, we engage in "small sins" that we don't intend to cause hurt, but they do. Gossip, unresolved conflicts, unchecked assumptions, refusal to talk to others, name-calling, revealing confidences—all these bend, bruise, and break our communities and ourselves.

Read James 3:1-12. James gives the congregation a tongue-lashing for their hurtful and intemperate comments, and claims without reservation that we cannot be praising God and building up the community at the same time we vilify and tear down someone else.

Earlier in his letter, James charged the same group with partiality toward the wealthy and disparagement of the poor (2:1-7); and he goes on to denounce them for having sold out to worldly values (4:1-10) and for their arrogant and self-serving behavior (4:13-17).

Lest he sound too harsh, James assured his hearers that there is tremendous blessing from snatching another soul from sin and restoring him or her to the way of truth (5:19-20). James knew that those of us who claim to be Christians have certain moral, ethical, and faithful codes to uphold and that we are judged by others on our fidelity to our beliefs. To do otherwise is to damage the community.

WHEN HURT HITS HOME

Someone has sinned against you. Or against your special someone. Or against your family, friends, fellow employees, schoolmates, or other form of community—lied, betrayed, insulted, shut out, committed violence. That hurts, and the more serious the sin, generally the more it hurts, sometimes in a life-altering way. It has been said that a healthier response to life's sometimes brutal events is not to say, "Why me?" but to ask: "What do I do now?"

We all hope for healing, although sometimes we are so hurt we don't expect it. Sometimes we so savor our wounds that we don't want healing, at least, not right away. And certainly, we cannot be so quick to leap to the language and expectation of healing that we fail to grieve adequately. Where do we find solace and healing, and when? Consider these personal stories.

Josh, Kenda, and Lin

Josh, Kenda, and Lin get together most mornings before work for coffee and socializing, generally about who's doing what with whom in the office. Since they don't always know the details, they speculate and share their "news" with coworkers. An employee who has been the frequent object of conversation was fired a few weeks ago. This morning Lin, Josh, and Kenda were named in a defamation and wrongful termination lawsuit brought against the company, and they have been summoned to explain themselves to their supervisors. Now *they're* the big story around the office,

DISCUSS

Look again at **When Hurt Hits Home.** Have you ever been in a situation that seemed so painful that you felt there was no way for the pain to subside or disappear? Have you ever savored your wounds so as to keep the hurt fresh? Have you ever been in a situation in which an attempt at healing or reconciliation was premature?

Discuss what happened, how you felt, and what resulted from those personal experiences. Was your community of faith a part of those experiences? If so, what difference did it make?

SMALL GROUP

If Another Sins Against You Gather several recent news magazines and newspapers. Search for and cut out headlines mentioning some of the extreme ways various communities across the world are injured or distorted (including natural disasters). Invite comments on the factors that allow these events to take place and to continue. Note that the issues are no doubt complex, so an easy fix is impossible. Nevertheless, brainstorm ways that reconciliation or restoration might take place. What issues would have to be faced? What would persons have to give up? have to risk? have to compromise? If religion or religious belief and practice have a part in the breach, how might those issues be addressed?

Read **Matthew 18:15-22** and examine the reconciliation process that Jesus outlined. Apply that process to one of the headlines or to one of the personal experiences mentioned earlier in the session. Could it work? Explain? What would it take to make it work?

The Search for Healing
Review this portion of the text. Form three groups. Assign to one **Leviticus 19–20**; to the second, **Matthew 18:15-22**; and to the third, **1 Corinthians 13**. Then respond to these questions:

■ What is the context of the passage?
■ To whom is it addressed?
■ What is the purpose?
■ What message comes to you today for your own life and for all the communities in which you live and move?
■ What are the spoken and unspoken "rules" in your various communities that establish boundaries and codify how you agree to live amicably? How are these rules made known to newcomers in the community?

Be sure to allow time for each group to report to the others a summary of their passage and of their discoveries.

and various other employees are already taking sides.

Carol and Larry

Carol and Larry have been married for three years. Their friends see them as a model couple, but Larry has a private violent streak, and he exercised it with a vengeance last night. He and Carol argued, and in an attempt to make up, Larry insisted that they make love. Carol wasn't ready for that kind of intimacy, but he forced himself on her. She feels violated but can't bring herself to face the word *rape*. Larry is, after all, her husband. In the midst of tremendous tension this morning, both of them are trying to sort out what happened and how to feel about it.

Fran, John, and Sally

Fran and John have a three-year-old daughter, Sally. They both have very busy jobs, so childcare is a necessity. But Sally seems to hate preschool—*any* preschool. She has a major tantrum every morning that often recurs during the day. Sally's teacher doesn't know what else to do and has suggested that Sally may need to be at home. John thinks that Sally will just grow out of it. Fran is considering staying at home, but they need both incomes. John doesn't want Fran to quit working or to start "rewarding" Sally for her crying. They are beginning to fight over the issue.

IF ANOTHER SINS AGAINST YOU

In Matthew 18, Jesus outlines a conflict resolution plan that, in successive stages, gives the aggrieved party and the sinner a way to heal the breach between them (18:15-19).

First is a face-to-face meeting. If that resolves nothing, the next step is to approach the offender with witnesses; then on to making the complaint public with the church. If none of these attempts at reconciliation is successful, the offender is to "be to you as a Gentile and a tax collector" (18:17).

Jesus is telling the community to expel the offender. If this were the end of the story, it would be cause for despair, or for justification to "purify" our communities of those who are different for any reason. But immediately following that passage, Jesus assures his followers that he is always among them to effect reconciliation (18:19-20) and that forgiveness is an ongoing process that never really ends (18:21-22).

THE SEARCH FOR HEALING

Expulsion from the community is not always the best plan for dealing with pain and breaches in community. Often enough, it is not up to us anyway. The ancient Israelite community had a plan too. Much of the Book of Leviticus contains rules and principles known as the Holiness Code (see, for example, Leviticus 19–20). Among other things, it deals with laws concerning clean and unclean food, animals, and people, and what has to be done to restore what is unclean to clean. Usually, the process involves making some kind of offering and ritual cleansing before the priest.

We may smile or yawn at what seem to be cultural, religious, or social anachronisms. But the point

SMALL GROUP

In pairs, take turns sharing one experience of injury or breach. It can be a personal or group experience, one in which you were the injured party or the offender; it could be a situation since resolved or never resolved. Whatever the case, be sure that the conversation stays only between each pair.

Discuss how the accountability was handled and by whom or what circumstance. Then talk about how the first step was taken to try to effect healing. Did prayer or some other faith dimension have a place? Who reached out first? What prevented reconciliation from starting or finishing? With the help of the faith community or of faithful practices, what might be done to effect healing now?

When Things Go Bad

Closing
You have had several opportunities to share very personal and painful experiences. Be sure to close with prayer. In your circle prayer, offer requests for healing, for understanding, for patience, and for love for each person.

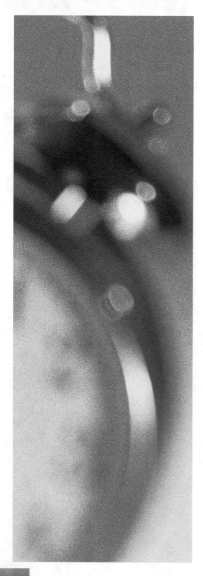

is that the Israelites had a process for restoring and renewing whatever was not right with the community. Generally they did this in the context of their worship with the community of faith. This included prayer, confession or presentation of oneself to the religious leader, and an offering.

These two processes—"repurification" in the context of the worshiping community; and reconciliation, personally or with other members of the community—affirm that the faith context is central in healing breaches in the community. We often have some kind of code or rules for how we live amicably—and how we settle our differences—even if those rules are unconscious or unstated. For Christians, the core of these rules is love, including the "tough love" of Matthew 18 that helps hold each of us accountable to others and the gracious spiritual gift of love in 1 Corinthians 13 that helps us understand how to be accountable to ourselves. In any case, we are ultimately accountable to a God of justice, grace, and mercy.

A FINAL WORD

Volumes have been written on grief, forgiveness, reconciliation, and healing. The principles sound easy enough, but often prove much harder in the doing. So it is important to remember that the first step is to *take* the first step, whatever it is. The next steps often work themselves out, especially with the help of caring members of the community—your family, your friends, your church, your coworkers, your fellow students—and certainly in prayer.

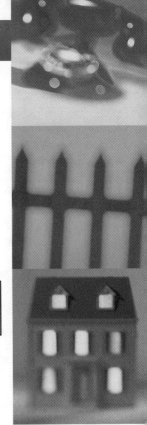

A PLACE IN THIS WORLD

> This session will address the questions, Where do I fit in? What can I give to others? What is God's plan for my life?

WHERE DO I FIT IN?

We all belong to some community or other, unless we live a completely isolated life. We have examined so far our communities of friends, family, family of faith, work, school, and primary relationships. And we have taken a beginning look at what happens when our communities suffer pain or distortion and how to begin working toward healing. Now we will pay special attention to integrating our thoughts about these communities and where we fit in, and what contribution we make.

This is a basic life question and an ancient one. From your study of Adam and Eve in Session 6, you might even say that the temptation of the first man and woman was rooted in their quest to "fit in" better by becoming like God. Suffice to say, we were created to be communal creatures, and we need to understand our place in the scheme of things. The question in some form surfaces time and again in the Bible.

Getting Started
In pairs, spend a few minutes reviewing the various communities of which you are a part and one major role you have in them.

A Man of Two Cultures

Skim back over Exodus 1–3 to remind yourself of the highlights from Moses' birth to his call by God. In what ways was Moses an insider and an outsider in his two cultures? How did he fit in (or not)? How did God use Moses' bicultural identity for God's purposes?

Have you experienced being in more than one culture at the same time? Did you feel as if you belonged? What did you do to help yourself feel at home? Who helped or hindered that process? What happened?

A MAN OF TWO CULTURES

Moses was a man of two cultures, complicated by the fact that the two cultures were at serious odds with each other. He was raised as an Egyptian, the enslaver of his cultural family. As a Hebrew, he empathized with the plight of his people. At a crisis point, Moses simply ran away (Exodus 2:11-15). He didn't stay away, because "after a long time," God sent him back as their deliverer (2:23-25; 3:7-10).

How did Moses fit into his communities? As son and leader, both in Egypt (as the adopted grandson of Pharaoh) and as the designated man of God, chosen to lead a nation from slavery to the Promised Land. He was also husband and father, both to his wife and children, but also as "surrogate" father to the children of Israel, who felt lost and alone during their journey.

THE SON OF MAN

The Son of Man

"Party" with Jesus. In small groups, choose one or more of Jesus' social engagements and examine how he interacted with other members of his family and community. How did he seem to feel in these situations? Does this provide any further insight into Jesus' life or personality for you? When you take Communion, can you envision Jesus at the wedding as well as at the last Passover meal? If so, what new light does that shed on table fellowship for you at church? at other social gatherings?

Jesus highlighted the fact that as the Son of Man, he "had nowhere to lay his head" (Matthew 8:18-20). His place was no place and every place. During his ministry, others sought to define or to keep him in his place, ("Is not this the carpenter's son?), and they took offense at him. Jesus' response: "Prophets are not without honor except in their own country and in their own house" (13:54-58).

He did find welcome in many a house, however, and we see him enjoying neighborhood celebrations, such as the wedding in Cana (John 2:1-12); as a dinner guest of Martha, Mary, and Lazarus (12:1-3) and many others; and as the host at Passover with his disciples (John 22:7-13). Jesus did ordinary "life things" with his family and his friends.

THE INNER CIRCLE OF JESUS

In terms of membership in the community of faith, Jesus warned that there is a cost for this discipleship (Mark 8:32-38). He warned his disciples that for his sake, they would endure family hostilities and other perils from an unbelieving community (13:9-13). Those who endure to the end will be saved.

The disciples did not always know how they fit in; James and John squabbled or competed for a special place with Jesus (Mark 10:35-45) and received a mild scolding for their efforts. They didn't quite understand what they were asking for, but they stayed together even after the Crucifixion to figure it out.

The Inner Circle of Jesus
Look up **Mark 10:35-45**. What were James and John asking for, and what was Jesus' response? Do you think their request was appropriate? (In other accounts, their mother made the request for them. Would that make any difference in your answer?)

Have you ever tried to fit in somewhere where you legitimately did not belong, at least at that time? What was that experience like? Did you find a way to exit gracefully? What did you learn?

How did they fit into their communities? They were "common" folk, for the most part; some were married, with business interests. They engaged the community where they were and drew on the familiar images of the day to spread their message.

SMALL GROUP

Fitting in the "Unfit"

Divide the three Scripture passages among three small groups. Use a Bible commentary to help uncover the great richness of these stories. First try to find out the position of each of these key figures in his or her community.

Examine how Jesus interacted with them. Use a creative way to do this examination, for example as a dramatization, or as a reporter interviewing the main character. Then join the groups together and discuss how Jesus fit in with the "unfit" and how he "refit" them into their own communities. What difference does your relationship with Jesus Christ make in terms of how you see yourself fitting into your various communities?

FITTING IN THE "UNFIT"

Jesus loved to fit himself in where "good" people didn't fit. There are numerous stories of Jesus eating with "tax collectors and sinners" (such as Zacchaeus in Luke 19:1-10); interacting with lepers, the most unclean and reviled among the community (such as in Luke 17:11-19); and engaging foreigners (such as the Samaritan woman in John 4:1-42).

In placing himself in the midst of the "unfit," he demonstrated wide boundaries of love and acceptance, redefining for the Jews the meaning of community and who "belonged." Just as important, Jesus' interaction also helped to reintegrate those persons into their own communities where they most likely had been marginalized or outcast.

DISCUSS

Think of your own experiences on either side of this situation: as the one who didn't fit and as the one who helped another fit in. How did it feel as the misfit? as the one who helped out? What did you learn from being in each position? What spiritual insight, if any, did you gain?

NO CRISIS OF CONFIDENCE

The apostle Paul seemed very sure of his place: "If anyone else has reason to be confident in the flesh, I have more." Then he went on to brag about his "pedigree," declaring himself "as to righteousness under the law, blameless" (Philippians 3:4b-6). Yet his life was not easy, and although his place was far from secure, he boasted about his beatings, shipwrecks, stoning, and other

BIBLE

No Crisis of Confidence
Look first at Paul's statement of his credentials in **Philippians 3:4b-6**. Read a bit further to see what his purpose was in bringing it up. Was it just to brag? If not bragging, then what?

Next, look at the ways Paul says he tried to adapt (1 Corinthians 9:19-23) so that he would meet his goal of sharing and spreading the gospel. How do you understand his accommodations to others in this light? his "boasting"? What does this say about the need for flexibility in our relationships and communities?

hardships as a sign of the success of his ministry (2 Corinthians 11:21-29). If there was that much opposition to it, he must have been doing something right! Paul fit in with everyone he could in order to spread the gospel (1 Corinthians 9:19-23). He understood his gifts and skills and used them with confidence.

GOD'S GOOD GIFTS

Just as Paul seemed very secure in his own gifts, he spoke at length about gifts and interdependence among members of the body of Christ. First, he was confident that we all have an equal place in the community; there are no special distinctions, in spite of the way we erect barriers based on class, creed, or nationality (Galatians 3:27-28). "All are one in Christ Jesus."

Second, whether very gifted or modestly talented, we all have a place of honor in the body. In fact, those with "lesser" gifts are to be more highly esteemed, and no one can attempt to edge out another as inferior. In the body, one of us may be an "eye," another a "hand"; and where would we be if the "ears" decided the body didn't need its "feet" (1 Corinthians 12:12-31)? This passage is part of a longer discourse on spiritual gifts (Chapters 12–14) that includes the wonderful passage about the centrality of love (Chapter 13).

DISCUSS

When have you had to bend to fit in with a particular group? If it felt unnatural, did that mean it was inappropriate? Explain. Under what circumstances is it acceptable to "become someone else" in order to get along in a particular place?

Persons in minority cultures have to bend and accommodate all the time and are much more familiar with the majority culture than the majority is with their culture. What do you think about this? Does Paul have anything to say to you about that? Explain.

SMALL GROUP

God's Good Gifts
Form groups of no more than four or five. Read 1 Corinthians 12:12-31. Briefly discuss it together to be sure everyone understands it. Then choose a body part (including some Paul did not name, if you wish). Try to match it to some gift of yours. For example, if you are good with tools, be the hands; or if you are a good listener, be an ear. Then explain to the rest of the body why your part is important, what it brings to the whole body, and why it is necessary. Keep this in mind for the next activity.

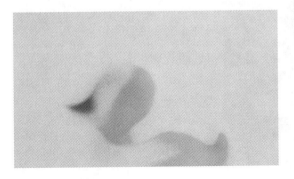

WHAT DO I HAVE TO OFFER?

This question is answered at least in part by examining our gifts. In previous chapters of this study, we mentioned that we have our own role to play in the communities in which we circulate. Those roles are often based on our gifts.

We are usually good at the things we enjoy and enjoy what we're good at. Just examining our likes and dislikes can help us zero in on our spiritual gifts. Paul mentions several tasks as spiritual work (1 Corinthians 12:27-30; Ephesians 4:11-13) and several characteristics as the "fruit of the Spirit" (for example, Galatians 5:22-23).

"What do I have to offer?" you ask. Well, what are your gifts?

You Want Me to Do *What*?

The chairperson of the nominating committee at church called and asked you to work with [the missions committee, a Sunday school class, the hunger program, the worship committee—you choose]. You haven't done this before, but you know you have the time if you care to use it that way. A colleague has been asked to assemble a team to work on a new project [starting a web page, working with United Way, an employee arbitration board or staff listener program, investigating the feasibility of an on-site day care center—you choose]. You have been invited to help, and your workload would permit it.

What will you do, and, more importantly, how will you decide?

WHAT IS GOD'S PLAN FOR ME?

Once you have an idea of your gifts, discerning God's plan for your life is much easier. If we accept that God gives us gifts to use for the benefit of God's kingdom, then it stands to reason that our gifts are the signposts along the path that God may want for us. In fact, we can't talk about how we fit into God's great scheme of things without a discussion of our gifts. However, we must also acknowledge that the path may, first of all, be a crooked one rather than direct; and second, that it may change.

What are the tools to help with this discernment? First, of course, is an examination of your skills, abilities, affinities, and loves. This examination should include an honest hearing from others. It is not so hard to either ignore or to overestimate our own gifts.

Second, examine your context. How do you relate to others? What communities do you participate in and in what capacity? Are you particularly pleased about how some tasks and relationships are working? especially frustrated about anything? Do you feel right at home in some ways and unsettled or incomplete in others? Do some tasks or roles always seem to find their way to you? Are there roles or tasks that you have consistent difficulty in facing? These places, roles, and relationships and your level of satisfaction make up part of the picture.

Third, use the Scriptures as a guide. What does Paul say about the marks of spiritual work and lifestyle? What does Jesus teach about discipleship? What did the Bible characters (either real people or those in parables) do that Jesus commended? What did Jesus' preaching teach you about how to live and what to do?

DISCUSS

What Is God's Plan for Me?

Figuring out God's plan for your life is an evolving, changing process, not something that is "solved," even if, for example, you feel called to a particular life vocation from which you expect to retire.

Review the four stages in the discernment process and add others you think are important. Ask a volunteer who would be comfortable digging into this question with the group to talk through steps one, two, and three. You have already done some thinking on step one and can be thinking about your own life even if you don't discuss it.

SMALL GROUP

Individually, or perhaps in pairs if couples or prayer partners wish to work together, take about five minutes of silence to pray about God's direction for you. You need not discuss this with anyone, but you may write down anything that comes to you for reflection much later.

Fourth, engage in prayer, including times of silence to let your mind go free enough to hear words or to see images that can be messages from God. Does some mental image, Bible verse, song lyric, or comment from a family member or friend keep coming back to you? Might there be a message in it for you?

The Restless Spirit

You are growing restless [at work, with your church responsibilities, with your school major—you choose]. It just doesn't feel right, but you haven't yet put a finger on why. You talk with a parent, who encouraged, even insisted, that you take on that responsibility. You also speak to your spouse or life partner, who wants you to do what you think is best; and to your best friend, who supports you but can't understand why you pursued that course to begin with.

Now what do you do?

A FINAL WORD

Finding your place and how to fit in to all the communities in which you participate can be a rocky and joyful adventure. Identifying what you have to offer to others can be a humbling and exhilarating experience. Discerning the direction God calls you to in life can be a scary and liberating process. But no matter what other circumstances you face, you are part of the Kingdom community; you have an important, respected, and necessary role in the body of Christ, and God will help you live it out.

The Restless Spirit

CASE STUDY

Form small groups of four or five. Seldom do we make all our decisions in isolation; others' opinions usually find their way into the mix. Choose your point of restlessness and work through what to do with the three different opinions about your situation. How do you decide who to listen to and what weight to give their contribution?

A Final Word

DISCUSS

Since this is the last session, you might want to have an *agape* meal or other form of ritual fellowship. You could invite the pastor to help you celebrate Communion. During this time, consider what this study group has meant to you, how it has become a place of community for you, and how (or whether) you will continue as a group.

Closing

CLOSE

After your ritual celebration, close with your circle prayer. Include prayers for the well-being of each group member in your various communities and for discernment in sharing your gifts within your communities.

CASE STUDIES

"Follow Me" (1)

Carmen is one of the smartest people you know. She is pleasant, caring, and generous. People tend to gravitate to her for advice and do not fear having their vulnerabilities exploited. Carmen has a vision for [a new congregation, business, way of working within your company—you choose] that you find very exciting. This venture is not without risk, however, and you would have to give up some important things [by relocating, investing your savings, taking a demotion—you choose] if you wanted to participate. Several others that you know are considering this adventure. Some of them seem to be persons who you think just can't get it together. Others are from very different backgrounds from you; some are your good friends. This morning, Carmen invited—even encouraged—you.

- What must you consider before committing yourself?

- How can you tell if this vision is attainable, sustainable, and right for you?

- What adjustments or compromises might you have to make?

- How would you need to work, do you think, to focus on a truly shared vision together?

- How would you form a community around this vision?

"Kevin and Stacy" (2)

Kevin and Stacy are married and are two of your best friends. Kevin has been like a brother to you since high school, and you have always felt that you can confide in Stacy no matter what the issue.

While having lunch in a restaurant one day, you spot Kevin with another woman. When you approach their table to say hello, Kevin seems strangely uncomfortable. He drops by your house later, and he asks you not to mention the incident to Stacy. When you ask why, Kevin simply says that he "wouldn't want Stacy to be hurt by this."

When you see Kevin and Stacy together again, they seem happy, and it is as though nothing has happened. One month later, Stacy tells you she is worried that she and Kevin seem a little far apart right now. She says, "I don't know what it could be. I don't know what I'd do with myself without him."

- What are the issues here?
- Should you just "mind your own business"? What are the possible courses of action you could take in this situation? How might you make the situation better? How might you make things worse?
- How would you respond to Kevin as a friend? to Stacy? How can you be a friend to both?
- How would you respond if you tried to talk to Kevin but he kept avoiding you?
- To whom do you owe the higher degree of loyalty in this situation, Kevin or Stacy?
- What do you believe Jesus would do in this situation?

"The Malcontent" (4)

Kelly never misses an opportunity to badmouth the job—the administration "doesn't have a clue," coworkers are just "out for themselves," the office equipment is "from the Dark Ages," and the food in the cafeteria is "worse than airline food." Yet Kelly is a gifted worker, efficient, and cooperative—even helpful—most of the time. She frequently takes on the tasks that no one else seems willing to do (though she complains about it). But the task is always done well. In spite of this good work record, most of your colleagues are reluctant to volunteer for specific tasks involving Kelly.
Today your boss taps you for a key role in a special project that Kelly will lead.

- How do you feel about this assignment? What are the best and worst possibilities here?

- How does your own sense of vocation for your work mesh with Kelly's apparent negativism? How can you deal with that attitude?
- Imagine that you have asked Kelly about her own job satisfaction. What response might you get?
- If job satisfaction is low when skills are high, what might be the point of disconnection?
- If your own job satisfaction is low or if you do not have a sense of calling for your own work, what might the combination of your attitude with Kelly's do to the task at hand?

"School Shooting" (6)

There has been a school shooting in your community. Three students and a teacher were killed, and several students were wounded—some seriously. The shooters, two teenage students, are in police custody. An investigation is underway into school security and the handling of the incident by school officials. Local and national media are here and are interviewing anyone who will talk.

You know many of the people involved:

- the teacher—He or she was your favorite teacher when you were in school;
- the victims—You are friends with their parents, they've been close friends with your children, or you belong to the same church or community group as they;
- the shooters—One of them attends your church, where his parents are also members.

This tragedy is tearing your community apart. People are looking for others to blame—the shooters; their friends; their parents; school officials; the educational system; the police; Satan; God; anyone. The incident has prompted a televised community meeting, and you decide to attend.

- What issues do you see here?
- What are some examples of negative or harmful responses that might occur?
- What are some examples of positive or helpful responses that might occur?
- What can the different characters do to help this community heal? What can you do?
- What do you believe is the role or response of God in this tragedy?
- You have the opportunity to speak out at the community meeting; what would you say?

Fill in or change details as you desire and continue to discuss. Or let each group member assume the role of a different character and engage in dialogue. Focus on listening as much as speaking. Try to identify both negative and positive comments and reactions, and look for ways to heal relationships and restore community.

SERVICE LEARNING OPTIONS

Consider undertaking some of the projects mentioned below to enhance your study of the biblical idea of community. You may find them transformational as well as helpful.

IDEA #1: Get Involved in Habitat for Humanity

Habitat for Humanity International is a nonprofit, ecumenical Christian organization that has provided adequate, affordable shelter for more than 80,000 families worldwide. Volunteers with no prior house-building experience or skills can donate time, money, and/or labor and work side-by-side with members of the family for whom the home is being built. Check with your church or community group, or at your place of work, to find out how they may already be partnering with Habitat; or lead the way by working with your pastor or group leader to get your church or organization involved. Use the white pages of your local telephone directory or an Internet search engine to locate a Habitat for Humanity affiliate near you.

IDEA #2: Do a Generational History Project

Design and organize a generational history project in your church or community. Interview older persons and any others who can relate stories and details of past people, places, and events of importance in the life of your church or community. Get volunteers to serve as organizers, planners, interviewers, and writers. Publish the results in your church newsletter, bulletin, or special booklet; or make this a full-scale presentation by using audio/visual equipment to produce a video documentary that the entire group can contribute to and enjoy. Try to provide an opportunity for every member of the church or community to get involved in some way.

IDEA #3: Help Someone Learn to Read

More than twenty percent of adults read at or below a fifth-grade level. Volunteer your time and talents as a teacher or tutor to help an adult learn to read, write, and/or speak English. Contact the National Institute for Literacy in Washington, DC, for information; or check the business pages of your local phone directory for a literacy group near you.